Y0-BPW-529

Simple
Money

Simple money-lessons for an extraordinary life

by **William Bell,** CFP, CLU, RHU

Copyright © 2007 by William Bell. All rights reserved. No part of this work covered by the copyrights herein may be reproduced or used in any form or by any means – graphic, electronic or mechanical, including photocopying, recording, taping or information storage or retrieval systems – without the prior written permission of William Bell, author.

Any request for photocopying, recording, taping or information storage or retrieval of the book shall be directed in writing to billbell@bellfinancial.ca Re: Simple Money permissions.

Care has been taken to trace ownership of copyright material contained in this text. The publisher will gladly receive any information that will enable them to rectify any reference or credit line in subsequent editions.

23rd Street Press
15165 Yonge Street Suite 201
Aurora, Ontario
Canada, L4G 1M1
www.bellfinancial.ca

National Library of Canada Cataloguing in Publication Data
Bell, William, 1957
         Simple Money

ISBN 1-55383-173-0

Note: *Simple Money* contains the opinions, thoughts, and ideas of the author. It is sold with the understanding that the publisher is not engaged in rendering professional services. If professional advice or other expert assistance is required, the services of a competent professional person should be sought.

Publication credits:
Cover: Jeff Thorsteinson, The Newsletter Factory
Book jacket photography: Anita Guttelaro, The Photographic Group, Aurora, ON
Printer: Friesens, Manitoba, Canada
Printed and Bound in Canada

Dedication

To Mom, **Phyllis I. Bell**

My life continues to be shaped by the valuable lessons you taught me, among them this:

"Money is **important**, but it's certainly not **most important."**

Table of Contents

Introduction and Acknowledgements

The idea for *Simple Money* began as an expansion of the "lessons" I use in trying to help clients understand the various financial issues that we all encounter. Most of these lessons have been repeatedly outlined on a white board, or a blank sheet of paper, and have served very well in illuminating the topic, fleshing out questions, and ultimately guiding us to the right decision. It seemed logical to summarize each of those lessons in a book. Sure, it appeared simple enough – about four years ago – when the idea was first discussed. As it turned out, it has been anything but simple.

Distilling ideas into a condensed form to create an "everything-you-need-to-know" book that is both complete and simple to understand isn't easy. I have frequently wondered why that didn't occur to me at the beginning.

The initial catalyst for this project was one of my partners, **David Frank.** We discussed the concept together and both agreed it was a good idea. I might have forgotten about it, but David did not. He kept reminding me how valuable this book could ultimately be to our clients, and in doing so, he inspired me to keep it moving forward – if ever so slowly. He has also contributed to many chapters by reading and editing, adding not only his abilities as a writer, but also as a skilled practitioner in financial services.

Even so, for almost two years, this project remained in my head. It was my attendance at a seminar sponsored by Manulife Financial and run by **Jeff Thorsteinson** (of YouFoundation and The Newsletter Factory) that created some momentum. I was sufficiently impressed by Jeff's understanding of the financial services industry to follow up with him, and we quickly discovered some common ground for a potential relationship – Jeff had helped other advisors produce books, and I was an advisor/author struggling for some guidance, and a big push.

For the past two years Jeff has been my "coach." He created a timeline, (which I of course failed to adhere to), and set up a process to draft, edit, refine and produce what has ultimately become this book. Our regular meetings (usually by phone as Jeff lives in B.C., and I live in Ontario), and his constant encouragement have been invaluable sources of guidance and inspiration.

One of the members of Jeff's team is **James Dolan**, an obviously skilled writer and incredible source of knowledge on a diverse list of topics, most notable among them, financial services. James edited my work with the zeal of a university professor, tirelessly correcting my oft-repeated mistakes, cleaning up my sentence structure, clarifying my thoughts, and asking questions that would always lead to a better way of explaining the idea at hand. My highest praise for James is this: This is a far better book, and more notably I have become a better writer, thanks to his work.

Throughout the past four years, a constant obstacle has been my lack of interest in writing a "textbook" – a dry series of facts and information, intended more as a reference than a source of inspiration. This is in large part the reason why for most of the time I have been working on this book, I have referred to it as "Simple Money Extraordinary Life." And my belief, as it is in working with clients, has *always* been: put money into its proper place, and an extraordinary life will emerge.

There are of course many others to whom I owe my gratitude for helping me with *Simple Money.*

Thanks to everyone at Bell Financial for their constant support: **Sonia, Cheryl, Zoe, Dawn, Wendy, Jean-Marc, Danny, Gerald, Geoff, Chad, David, Laurie, Ellen, Suzanne**, and especially **Gloria,** who has faithfully included time in my week to work on "the book" without ever losing faith that it would be time well spent.

Countless people I work with, including our partners at **Manulife Financial, Mackenzie Financial, Fidelity Investments, AIM Trimark Investments, CI Investments, Franklin Templeton Investments, Saxon Mutual Funds, Capital International Asset Management, RBC, TD Mutual Funds, Northwest Mutual Funds, Vengrowth Capital Management, Great West Life** and others, have provided important encouragement by regularly asking, "So, how's that book coming?"

Thanks to **Robert Gignac** and **Lorraine Greey** for reviewing our close-to-final copy, catching a number of errors, and making numerous great suggestions.

Thanks to **Joanne Thomas Yaccato,** for validating my beliefs about how financial services should be delivered, and for lending her important support to this project by writing some brief words of introduction.

A huge thanks to **Ted and Susan Chant,** whose friendship and willingness to help have been instrumental in bringing this project to fruition.

The relationship that all of us at Bell Financial share with **our clients** is a constant source of pleasure and pride. But I know I am particularly blessed to be able to share in the discovery and pursuit of the most important dreams of so many wonderful people. I thank you most sincerely for inviting me into your lives. Some of you may find a part of our story together in the pages of this book. Rest assured that names and circumstances have been sufficiently changed to ensure your identity is not revealed. In fact, in most cases the facts are combined with those of another client to further obscure your identity – perhaps even from yourself.

And of course, I want to acknowledge my family. My three girls, **Leah, Deandra, and Alexis,** never cease to amaze me. You are wonderful, dynamic, caring people, already living extraordinary lives. And **my wife, Ellen,** whose love I treasure more than anything; you are my everlasting muse.

All four of you inspire me. But in truth, I believe you actually slowed the process of writing this book. Many a day I had set aside for working on this book ended up being spent with you instead.

And my life has been **extraordinary** because of it.

Foreword

by Joanne Thomas Yaccato
President and founder of The Thomas Yaccato Group
Author of: *Balancing Act: A Canadian Woman's Financial Success Guide*, *Raising Your Business: A Canadian Woman's Guide to Entrepreneurship*, and *The 80% Minority: Reaching the Real World of Women Consumers*.

Perspective.

Such a simple concept. Alas, but not when it comes to money.

It's been my experience that the majority of Canadians who fall off the rails when planning their financial futures do so because of the lack of "perspective." I've seen it time and time again. Those who achieve what they want in life do so because they've done the work around understanding the role money plays in their life. They take the time to gain perspective.

That's what separates this book from the pack. While you will learn the nuts and bolts of financial planning, it departs from the usual drill by revealing that it all won't amount to a hill of beans if you can't find some way to make it all relevant to your life.

And that's the gift of this book.

It has the effect of slowing us down, taking a deep breath, clearing our head and thinking. This book offers everything people need to make sound decisions and in an accessible way. (You'll hear Bill's voice in your head…) But what I embraced

v

was the one essential step most people (including financial advisors) miss when creating a financial plan: It's not a math exercise. If this is going to work, then we need to take the time to dig deep and figure out our relationship with money.

It's rare to find advice in a book that is so real-life. There's no chastising or judgment. There is no right-way or wrong-way.

It's about finding our own way.

Joanne Thomas Yaccato

Simplifying money for
an **extraordinary** life

With a solid understanding of the basic tools of personal finance, and freed from the belief that there is only one way to the perfect future, we all can live our lives to the fullest.

Simple.

Not a word often applied to financial matters and yet a noble goal in an increasingly complex world. We long for things to be simple – not as in "let's all go back to the horse and buggy days," but in a "hey, I really understand that" sense.

Extraordinary.

When it comes to describing a life, this word is generally reserved for those who climb mountains, cure diseases, or build empires. Yet all of us long to break out of the ordinary lives we see before us. We hope to experience more, have more, and be more than we are right now. And we wonder how to make that possible.

As a financial planner, I get to ask people about their dreams – about their vision for an "extraordinary life." It's fun work. It's also discouraging. Most people have trouble coming up with anything that would be described as truly extraordinary. More of the same is what most people want to plan for. Backsliding into poverty is their greatest fear.

Some, however, do plan for the extraordinary. They want to travel, spend more time with family, fix up an old car, read the classics. Some want to change careers – not to make more money, but to find greater fulfillment. Many want to relocate – bigger house, smaller house, quieter neighbourhood, a view of the lake, more land. Dreams come in all sizes.

It's invigorating to listen to people talk about what they *really* want. And disappointing to find out that those dreams are pinned to the hopes of winning the lottery.

Some regard money as the great enabler of dreams. They seem to have all they need to pursue the life they imagine. For most however, money is the great *disabler* of dreams – the number one reason why they don't take the next step towards their version of the "extraordinary life."

It **needn't** be so.

Money is simply *one* tool in our toolbox to help us get things done. But money has become so important in our lives – and so complex – that we have gradually forgotten about all the other tools. We focus all of our efforts on acquiring and understanding money to the detriment of other, more important parts of our lives.

I won't dispute that money is an important matter if one wishes to live in the civilized world. Clearly, it can't be ignored. But I would argue that it is not nearly as deserving of the attention that it currently receives in the media, on the street, and in the minds of most Canadians. It needn't be all-consuming.

For most people, a definition of an extraordinary life would probably include "never worrying about money." Since you can't ignore money, then the goal must be to reduce it to its essentials. To know enough to make good choices, but not so much as to get bogged down in financial details.

To pursue your dreams, to live an extraordinary life, you need to have money work for you, and then get out of the way. Let me illustrate by introducing you to the Smiths and the Breens.

The Smiths and the Breens

Nancy and Bob Smith are a typical Canadian couple. They have two children and a dog. They live in the suburbs and they bring in a respectable income. They are paying down their mortgage. They're saving enough to put the kids through university, and to retire comfortably in their early 60s. They take vacations annually, always managing to stay within their budget. They are, in their own words, "not wealthy, but comfortable." Nancy would love to have a pool but neither she nor Bob wants to commit to the expense.

Lisa and Mike Breen are also a typical Canadian couple. And in many respects, they are quite similar to the Smiths. They too have two kids and a pet (a cat). They too live in the suburbs. And they bring in almost exactly the same income as the Smiths. However, they feel that they are "in a financial mess." Their annual vacations always manage to go over budget. They are tormented by debt. They are worried they aren't saving enough for the children's education or for their own retirement. They feel insecure and troubled. Financial stress is making them unhappy today, and they hold little hope that their financial future is going to be any better. They do, however, have a pool.

In truth, the financial picture for the Smiths and the Breens is remarkably similar. The amount of money they spend is almost the same. Their net worth – at the moment at least – is virtually the same as well. They are in fact *both* on track to put the kids through school and retire in comfort.

Why then do they *feel* so differently about their respective financial situations?

The Smiths and the Breens are essentially two families in similar financial positions, looking forward and imagining two *different* worlds. Their beliefs and perceptions about money change what they expect from life.

In a very real sense, our lives are shaped by our *perception* of money. Many of the day-to-day decisions we make, the goals we set for ourselves, and especially the material possessions or experiences we deny ourselves, are a result of what we *believe* about money.

It may appear that the "rules of money" are universal, but the place it holds in each of our lives is unique. And so when we compare ourselves to others, or listen to the talking heads on the television, or read the magazine article that tells us what we should or shouldn't be doing with our money, more often than not we become confused. Our problem isn't lack of information – it's that we have too much of the *wrong* information, and no way of sorting out the facts from fiction, and truth from perception.

We need to sift through the mountain of information and discover the *simple* facts about money. We need to stop looking for right and wrong. Should I invest or pay down debt? Should I invest in equities or fixed income? Should I buy universal life or term life insurance? These and countless other financial questions all demand the same answer – "it depends." And not just on your personal circumstances, but on your *personality*.

Simply put, it would be a mistake to assume that the Smiths have it right and the Breens have it wrong. Or vice-versa. The Smiths place a great deal of importance on appreciating the value of a dollar. Hard work, careful saving, and sensible spending are at the core of their financial personalities. The Breens, on the other hand, place a higher value on expanding their horizons. They're more interested in "living life to the fullest." And in order to do that, they believe some money must be spent, and some financial risks must be taken.

And while you may think that the Smiths are calm, cool, and collected when it comes to money, nothing could be further from the truth. The Smiths see their friends using money to enjoy life now, and they worry that perhaps they are missing out! The Breens worry that by living fully now, they may suffer at some point in the future. Both worry about money, and yet for remarkably different reasons!

Is either couple living an
"extraordinary life?"

Not according to Nancy Smith. Why? Well there's the pool of course, but there are other things as well. The Smiths enjoy their vacations, but would like to be able to take the children on more extravagant trips to Europe and other parts of the world. And as much as it appears that their financial world is in complete control, they still feel that money rules their lives far too much. When I asked them to create a vision of their future in which they had all the money they could possibly need, Bob and Nancy were both at a loss. They were unable to look outside their present financial circumstances because they saw no alternative as *possible*.

The Breens on the other hand were easily able to describe their perfect future – and it involved a lot more money. With very little thinking they started talking about a cottage, a bigger house, private school for the children, more frequent vacations, golf memberships, and more. The Breens were determined not to let money stand in their way, and so they were willing to take bigger risks. Mike's career had taken many turns as he climbed the corporate ladder, jumped and climbed again. Their investments tended to be aggressive, causing them to ride waves of giddy exhuberance when things were up and dive deep into a well of depression when things went down. They willingly accepted debt as a long term reality, taking on more and more in order to finance the things they wanted. It had become normal for them to live in a state of uncertainty with respect to money. But that didn't mean they liked it.

The Smiths' "extraordinary life" ultimately involves taking more risks and coming to terms with the realization that it is okay *and* possible to want more than they have now. They should get the pool, and they should take the children to Europe.

The Breens' "extraordinary life" involves setting priorities, and simplifying their finances so that they can understand how they are going to get to their various destinations. They need to gain more confidence in long term strategies in order to believe that current spending isn't going to upset long term goals.

What both the Smiths and the Breens need in order to achieve their future goals is *clarity* about how money works for them, and how it can be used to accomplish their respective goals. The Smiths will spend more freely if they see that their future goals are in fact being accomplished, and they may start dreaming bigger when they see the power of long-term investing. The Breens will feel more relaxed if they can understand how much risk they truly need to take, and stop taking risks simply for the sake of making a quick buck. Confidence in their long-term goals will reduce the financial stress that is taking the fun out of the good life they are already enjoying.

Both families don't need a lot of information, they just need to understand it. In other words, they need *simplicity.* They have some similar questions about investing, life insurance, RRSPs, taxes, education savings, cash management, and other financial topics. They don't want to become "experts," they just want to know how these basic tools work and how those tools may or may not be important to *them.* Then they can prioritize according to their unique situations and put all the pieces together. They can stop wondering if they are in fact on the right track, and move ahead with confidence.

That's what this book is **all about.**

Each of the chapters in this book will deal with a specific financial topic. I'll begin by providing a brief history of the subject to help us gain perspective on why we believe certain things about money today. Next, I'll provide a simple lesson which distills all you really need to know about the topic at hand. The chapter will conclude with a discussion on how and where to apply this lesson. Throughout you will find a sprinkling of real life situations drawn from my experiences working with real life people, as well as a healthy dose of supplemental information intended to answer your questions as they arise, and add depth to the main ideas of the chapter.

You may not see yourself in the Breens or the Smiths, or for that matter in any of the other people whose lives you will read about in this book. But don't think you can't learn from their stories.

You don't have to be a mechanic to drive a car. But you should know how to put gas in the tank, and air in the tires. Similarly, you don't need to be a financial expert to be able to use money effectively. But you should understand the basics of your important decisions – how to save, how to invest, and how to protect yourself from financial hazards.

If the content of this book constitutes all you know about money, it should be enough. A bold statement perhaps, but in fact, this is the essential point of this book. The most important step you can take towards an extraordinary life is simply to let go of the financial information you don't need – the ideas and beliefs that are holding you back.

With a solid understanding of the basic tools of personal finance, and freed from the belief that there is only one way to the perfect future, we all can live our lives to the fullest. Our goal should be to think very little about money and worry about it even less. We simply want to make smart financial decisions – decisions that can start us on the path towards the life we choose.

An extraordinary life that begins

right now.

Finding the starting point – visioning your **future**

Visioning your future is all about the extraordinary life. How you define that is up to you. But define it you must.

A brief historical perspective

Our thoughts give rise to our circumstances. Controlling the world around us is simply a matter of controlling the world within us. Moreover, without taking charge of our thoughts, we have no chance of making our dreams come true. While some may call this thinking "new age" or revolutionary, these ideas are as old as recorded history. Consider the following words of wisdom:

"The wisest men follow their own direction."
Euripides, (484 BC - 406 BC)

"Our plans miscarry because they have no aim. When a man does not know what harbor he is making for, no wind is the right wind."
Marcus Annaeus Seneca (59 BC – 39 AD)

"First say to yourself what you would be. Then do what you have to do."
Epictetus (55 – 135 AD)

"The world makes way for the man who knows where he is going."
Ralph Waldo Emerson (1803-1882)

"If one advances confidently in the direction of his dreams and lives the life he has imagined, he will meet with a success unexpected in common hours."

Henry David Thoreau (1817-1862)

"Dream lofty dreams, and as you dream, so shall you become. Your vision is the promise of what you shall at last unveil."

John Ruskin (1819 – 1900)

"The first essential, of course, is to know what you want."

Robert Collier (1884 – 1950)

"All of our dreams can come true, if we have the courage to pursue them."

Walt Disney (1901 – 1966)

These ideas were given new life with the onset of the industrial age. Figures like Andrew Carnegie and Henry Ford amassed fortunes and credited their success to attributes of the mind. Self-help literature for more than a hundred years extolled the virtues of "positive thinking," and lead us to the conclusion that we could "Think and Grow Rich."

The popular self-help literature of the past few decades has increasingly lead us on a journey inward. Today's highly respected authorities on this subject – people like Steven Covey, Wayne Dyer, and Deepak Chopra – are helping us see that accumulating wealth, while easily done, isn't the ultimate goal. We are finally realizing that the ultimate question is not how but why. Success is not found in achieving the goal, it's found in setting the right goal.

We may soon be **completely out of excuses** for why our life isn't exactly how we want it to be.

The simple lesson

Know what you want.

Here's a hint: it's not money. It may of course be what money buys. And money buys plenty: homes, cars, vacations, cottages, clothing, education, and an endless array of gadgets and toys.

So, what do **you** want?

I ask this question to every one of my clients. The sad reality is that almost no one has a clear answer. We don't know what we want. The most popular answer to the question is something like, "I just want to be able to continue to afford the life I have now." So what we want it might seem, is more of the same. Not very inspiring.

The lesson in this chapter is simply this: all that you want, all you could ask for, is yours for the taking. But first, you must know what it is.

Putting the lesson to work
to live the extraordinary life

It seems logical to accumulate the money first, and then decide what you are going to do with it after you have it. But this is precisely what keeps us on the treadmill, trying hard to stay where we are, fearing we might slip backwards.

A long list of experts point to the same conclusion. When you know what you want, when you have a clear vision of what you are pursuing, then all of the resources required, including money, will become available to make it your reality.

If you are like most people you are thinking to yourself, "My life isn't anything like I want it to be. How can this possibly be true?" Your problem isn't from a lack of applying this lesson. It's simply a

failure of **imagination.**

BEGIN WITH THE END IN MIND

This is Steven Covey's second in his famous list of *Seven Habits of Highly Effective People.* I always believed that logic dictated it should be first on the list, but it's his list. This is the essence of this chapter and a powerful idea. The key of course is finding "the end."

For some things the end is obvious. Buying a house, the end is closing day. Getting a degree, the end is graduation. Luckily, for the purposes of financial planning, goals that involve money almost always work into this neat format.

But not all the pieces of your vision statement may follow this example. Sometimes "the end" is much more elusive. You want a better relationship with your spouse for example, or you want to raise wonderful children. Where, exactly, is the end, and how do you measure your progress along the way?

In most of those cases, it serves best to consider the end as being either the end of your life (truly "the end,") or now. You may find it helpful to write your own eulogy, to be used at the end of a long and happy life. Many of the things you will hope are remembered about you will provide you with excellent clues regarding how you want to live your life today – especially with respect to the issues surrounding family and loved ones. Once you have "imagined" the very end, it will be easier to understand what you should do today. For example, if improving your most important relationship was your desire, ask: "If today my relationship were as I could imagine, how would I act?" You may be surprised to discover that this is a goal that can be accomplished literally now.

We live in a society that makes it hard for us to let our imagination out of the box. We are conditioned to like what others tell us to like. And others are telling us we would like (or need) a better car, a bigger house, and a new wardrobe.

The power in the vision exercise is in letting your imagination do the work it is intended to do. Designing and creating a world that expresses your true desires. You won't find those desires in a magazine or on television. They are where they have always been: inside. Here's how to get them out.

The big step – create a vision of your future

Create a vision of your ideal future. In your mind, project yourself ahead in time to the point at which you have "arrived." Who are you? What do you do? How do you spend your time? How do you spend your money? Who are you with? What have you accomplished? What are you most proud of? If you had all the money you needed to do whatever it is you would like to do, or have whatever it is you would like to have, what would those things be, and what would your life be like?

Write down your answers to all of these questions, and create a few paragraphs that paint a picture of that life. Write it in the first person present tense. For example, you might say, "I work three days per week at a job I love and spend the rest of my time with my family or on the golf course. We take two vacations every year to discover new countries and cultures. I am proud that we give generously to several charities and my church, and of the fact that I serve on the board for a charity."

Consider every aspect of your life, including your family, career, hobbies, friends, spiritual, charitable activities and any other activities you're involved with.

Don't limit yourself based on your current situation. Let your imagination and not your present circumstances define your limits.

Consider this document your "vision statement." It is a work in progress. You will never finish it, so don't be frustrated by the fact that it always appears to be unfinished. It's meant to be. There are things you can't yet imagine that will one day appear in your vision!

Read it often, and revise it. As you do, make it more specific – as specific as possible. For example, we may revise our first example to say,

> "I work Monday to Wednesday as an independent consultant for ABC Company. I love working with them, and I love being independent. I golf every Thursday and Saturday at my club – Golf

Haven, with my good friends Ron, Bob, and George. I shoot in the low 80s. I devote Fridays to volunteer with the Canadian Cancer Society and serve on their board. I am at home every evening and all day Sunday with my wife and children. We travel together every spring to somewhere warm and exotic, like Mexico, Jamaica, and Bermuda. Every summer we take two weeks to explore a new country, like Thailand, Australia, and England. We donate 5% of our gross family income to the Canadian Cancer Society and 5% of our gross family income is contributed to our Church."

Always ask yourself two things: (a) is this really what I want? And (b) can I be more specific and more descriptive? You may struggle with the words, but in your mind you should be able to get to the point at which you can play an imaginary "movie," starring you, of this future vision. Play this movie regularly.

Keep working on your vision and you will begin to see the world around you change in ways that sometimes defy explanation. Yet these changes will move you toward your ideal. Eventually you will see that through the process of visualizing the future you want, you are actually creating that future in the real world.

Setting Goals

For many the art of visioning is a big step. And a difficult one. That's why it's important to remember that it is a work in progress. The important thing isn't that you have vision statement that will rival the work of Shakespeare. The important thing is you have begun.

As you work on this vision statement ask yourself another important question. What should I do *next* in order to move me closer to this ideal? This will help identify your short term goals.

MEET MARTIN AND SARAH LINDEN

The easiest financial plan I have ever put together was with Martin and Sarah Linden. They were a newly married couple and came to me fairly certain that they needed a lot of help. They had big plans and they felt that their lack of financial knowledge was sabotaging them in their efforts to see their plans through.

When I asked the question, "So, what things do we need to plan for over the next several years?" I got an immediate and well-articulated response. By the time I finished scribbling down notes I realized I had just mapped out, in fairly fine detail, the next 10 to 15 years of their lives. They knew how many children (2), the kind of house (I remain convinced they already knew the address), how much money they would need to buy and carry the house (almost to the penny), the kind of education they wanted for their children (the costly kind) and the vacations they wanted to take (I didn't ask for an annual itinerary, but probably could have got one).

I was impressed. And a little frightened. I had never had clients come to me with such specific and considering their newly-wed status, such lofty dreams. I feared that perhaps they were "aiming too high." Shame on me for even thinking like that.

A list of their assets soon revealed that they were well on their way to accumulating what they needed. And their "lack of knowledge" had served them well. Most of their money was in high interest liquid accounts, as it should be. Their incomes weren't high, but sufficient, and both of them had ample room to grow. I saw no reason why every item on their carefully composed list wouldn't come true, in most cases, sooner than they expected.

The financial plan for them was like pushing down on the accelerator. Armed with a significant boost in the belief that they were headed in the right direction and doing the right things they forged ahead. We revisit and revise the plan regularly. Needless to say, their dreams are all coming true. They have a little girl and are expecting another in the summer. They live in a beautiful home. A cottage is now on the horizon. The fact that this planning exercise for me was so simple has made watching this extraordinary life unfold no less rewarding.

For example, your vision statement may say "We spend every weekend and all summer at our beautiful cottage on Lake Muskoka," while at the moment, you don't even own a cottage. So, start planning. How much will it cost? Determine what you will need as a down payment. Determine an appropriate time frame for you to accumulate those funds. This is when you will buy the cottage. Now you have a goal. Put that date on the calendar. Begin saving each month.

It's important to remember that goals are not your vision. They are steps toward the vision. Goals are important in that they allow us to break the journey into manageable steps. They help us determine and take the appropriate actions. They allow us to measure our progress. But they aren't the end of the road. There is no end of the road. The end is always changing, growing, and adapting.

Be specific

Go to the airport, walk up to the counter and tell the agent you want to buy a ticket to Europe.

"Where in Europe?" the agent will ask.

"Just Europe," you answer.

THE BRAIN AS A GOAL-SEEKING MECHANISM

Napoleon Hill wrote *Think and Grow Rich* in 1937. Maxwell Maltz wrote *Psycho Cybernetics* in 1960. Many other similar books have been written before, between and after these dates, but these two stand as perhaps the most widely read on the topic. Their premise is fairly simple. Our brains are wired to pursue whatever goals we put there. Want a new house? Imagine you already own it. See it clearly. Imagine yourself living in it. Involve all of the senses. Now look in the real world for the house you are imagining. It's out there. When you find it drive by it often and start to imagine you live there. (Be careful not to cross over the line of stalking the people who live there now.) It will eventually be yours. Your brain is powerless to do anything except deliver to you exactly what you "program" it to do. It might sound spooky and mysterious. But it works.

"But I need a specific destination. Europe is a big place!" the agent will say, likely in an exasperated voice, and probably looking around to make sure security is nearby.

The agent won't be able to help you unless you are specific, and then you will get a ticket that will take you to an exact location, a specific city and even a specific airport.

In the same way, your mind can't process destinations like "more money," "happier," "a nicer car," "a bigger house," or "a comfortable retirement." So, your mind does what the agent will eventually do if you persist in your decision to go to "just Europe." Your mind will decide to keep you just where you are.

Determine exactly what it is you want, and when you will have it. For example, you will be mortgage free (exactly zero dollars in debt), in fifteen years. Now get a calculator and determine what that means every month for the next 180 months.

Write it down

This is important for many reasons.

1. There is a different level of commitment made when you put things on paper.
2. Writing requires greater clarity of thought. Clarity is important.
3. You need to read and re-read, edit and re-edit. Unless you have a super-memory, writing it down is the only way.
4. Words in our head are still resident in our imagination. Words on paper are now part of the real world. This is an important transformation. This is *the* transformation.

THE POWER OF WRITTEN GOALS

A study done at Harvard in 1954 surveyed all of the students and found only 3% of the student body with goals that were written down. 20 years later, that 3% was worth more than the combined net worth of the other 97%. Seems they knew what they wanted.

Make it *your* future

Don't let someone else tell you what you want. Studies say that on average, we will need 70% of our current income in retirement. So what? What do *you* want to do in retirement? How much will that cost? Don't worry about being above or below average.

Be **you.**

Don't let marketing geniuses infiltrate your mind. Recognize that almost everyone is selling you something. Suppress jealousy and learn how to be happy for others. Focus on what you really want. Recognize that pursuing what others want or what others want you to want, is wasting valuable time, money and energy.

Tap into the power of belief

Some would say that your plans for the future need to be realistic. I don't like that choice of words. Realistic is a word that implies external judgment. There can be no external judgment on your vision of what can be. All progress is made by someone who believes in the impossible.

Belief is the word we are looking for here. You need to believe in your dreams. If you don't, you will sabotage yourself, or give up. But if you do believe, nothing can stop you.

MEET BELINDA BEST

Most advisors would have quickly dismissed Belinda Best as not worthy of becoming a client. She was over 40, single, in an average-paying job that she had held for over 10 years, and she had saved nothing other than the assets she was forced to save in her company pension plan. She wasn't in any financial trouble as she had no debt, but was naturally concerned that she might be headed for disaster if she didn't start saving for retirement.

It wasn't too hard to see that Belinda wasn't going to get very inspired about retirement as she was virtually unable to answer the standard "What do you want to do, and when do you want to do it?" question. She wasn't able to extend her vision out that far because there was a significant road block in between now and then. She wanted to own a home.

Belinda lived in an apartment, and while she had resigned herself to the fact that this was appropriate for her, she couldn't help but dream of owning her own place. She was simply unable to believe that she could afford it, and as time moved on and she did nothing about it, it seemed increasingly out of reach.

We put together a financial plan that focused on the next five years, and considered the financial choices that Belinda would have to make if she was going to have her own place. When she saw it in black and white she was noticeably excited. For the first time she was faced with the idea that her dream was in fact possible. She now even had someone else – a professional no less – telling her it looked like a good idea.

Over the next two years Belinda saved a considerable portion of her income and during the third year she purchased a new home. The home was to be built so that she could move in a year later. By closing day she had accumulated more than 25% of the purchase price and was easily able to carry the mortgage.

Shortly after her move she reflected on the transformation that had taken place in what seemed like a very short four year period. "I spent years believing I couldn't buy my own home. Now I have one." Her eyes sparkled. "I just focused all my energy and my thoughts into getting this house. And it worked." I could hear the wheels turning in her mind as she continued. "It's amazing what you can do when you put your mind to it!"

Indeed. Belinda is now focused on funding her retirement. A retirement filled with a number of things she had previously been unable to imagine. The extraordinary life that at one time appeared out of reach to Belinda is now for her remarkably simple to obtain.

How do you go from disbelief to belief? Sometimes slowly, one step at a time. It's okay to paint a vision of your future that is outside the realm of what you believe possible at the moment. You don't need to see how to get from here to there right now. You only need to believe that it's possible – someday. And you need to know which way to go next. What's the next move you can make that will move you closer? Take the step. Eventually you will take a step and find yourself understanding something for the first time: how to take the last step and get exactly what you want.

Find inspiration

Most New Year's resolutions last a few days or weeks at best. They tend to be things we think we should do – like lose weight, stop smoking, cut down on something – but they aren't things we find inspiring.

Inspiration cannot be handed to you by someone else. It isn't found "out there." It's only found inside. In answering the question, "What do I want?" some of the things on your list will make you feel something. It may be a kind of fear. It may be excitement. It is probably inspiration. Follow those things, whatever they may be.

Focus on what you do want, not what you don't want

Our minds are crammed with thoughts, and sadly, many of them are thoughts of what we don't want. When we think to ourselves, "I don't want to be in debt," or, "I hope I don't get fired," or "I don't want to fight with my spouse," not only are we taking up the space that should be occupied thinking about what we do want, we are also unintentionally bringing closer the very thing we fear. And one thing is certain. We will perpetuate our present state – the state of worrying.

It is important to let go of our fears. You can't possibly believe you are in control otherwise. And we need to turn all of our thoughts towards the realization of our ideal. So "I don't want to be in debt," is replaced with "I own my home outright." "I hope I don't get fired," becomes, "I love my job." "I don't want to fight with my

MEET RYAN AND ELAINE STEELE

Ryan and Elaine Steele are a happy couple living a fairly simple life. They have one child, Melissa, who is 9. Despite the fact that they live in urban Toronto and Melissa attends a local private school, they don't have an extravagant life. With a combined income of about $125,000 they managed to do all the things they found important, and still save regularly for their retirement and for Melissa's post secondary education. Their home was simple, but very warm and comfortable. I always enjoy visiting them because I feel like I have stepped out of the city and into a cottage in the country.

Our initial financial plan showed that they were easily on track to both retire only a few years after Melissa graduated. Ryan indicated that he enjoyed his work as a carpenter and would probably continue working much longer. Elaine indicated that she would probably retire as soon as possible. That was a red flag.

It was more than a year later that we got to the inevitable conversation about Elaine's career. She was the primary breadwinner, with her income of more than $90,000 per year. But, she wanted to go to school and retrain to become a naturopath, based on her belief in natural healing and interest in helping others. There were obvious problems with this plan. While she was in school the family would need to dip into savings in order to survive. And her new career would never generate her current income, meaning they would have to rethink their long term spending and make adjustments to lifestyle. To most people, it may have appeared impossible.

We reworked the financial plan and they looked at the numbers. With a few adjustments, it could be done. Ryan was completely supportive. He knew what it was like to actually enjoy what you do, and he wanted nothing less for Elaine. Melissa's private schooling remained a priority and so was still included in the projections.

For most of us, the number one obstacle stopping us from doing what we want is simply that we don't believe we can. The financial plan removed that obstacle for Elaine. She could no longer say it couldn't be done. And empowered now with the magic of belief she took the plunge.

That was five years ago. Today Elaine is a practicing naturopath, not surprisingly already more successful than she had hoped for. Both Elaine and Ryan are amazed at how effortless the financial adjustments seemed to be. But that's the amazing thing about knowing what you want. It's simple. And it's extraordinary.

spouse," becomes "I love my spouse and we get along wonderfully."
Stay **focused** and stay **positive**
and watch how much faster your ideal life materializes.

Visioning your future is all about the extraordinary life. How you define that is up to you. But define it you must. Know what you want. It isn't money. If the extraordinary life you imagine is going to materialize, money couldn't be much simpler, because money won't be an issue you give much thought to.

SIMPLE MONEY	EXTRAORDINARY LIFE
It's not money you want.	It's what the money *buys* that you want. What is that?
All the money you need to live the life you want will become available to you.	Put your imagination to work. Create a vision of your future that you can see, feel, taste, and hear. Write in the first person present tense. Revise it as often as you like.
	Write it down.
How much money will you need, and when?	Be specific.
	Find inspiration. It's in you.
	Believe. Only *you* need to believe in your dreams.
Let others worry about money. You don't need to.	Make it yours. Don't follow the dreams of others.

Chapter 3

Getting from **here** to **there** – financial **planning**

The key to the extraordinary life is to know these three simple things: where you are, where you are going, and what you should do right now to take you there.

A brief historical perspective

A recent job satisfaction study done in the U.S. rated "Financial Planner" at the top of the list. I'm delighted to be part of a group that garners such admiration. But I'm a little troubled by the reasons given for the ranking: lots of time off, and a high level of income. The truth is, the average consumer doesn't really know what a financial planner does, or how difficult it is. That's not surprising. The industry itself isn't sure either.

That may be harsh judgment, but I believe that it's a real problem with financial services at the moment. This is a young industry, and growth has been rapid and easy. Financial advisors of every description have simply been too busy to worry about mapping out a viable long-term business strategy for the industry.

As recently as the 70s, Financial Planning as a career was non-existent. If financial services was your chosen profession, you became a stock broker, a banker, an insurance agent or an accountant. Now, all of these professions are increasingly migrating to the title of Financial Planner. The lines that were once clear between these groups have all but disappeared.

A generation ago, if you wanted to do something that required a large sum of money – for example take a vacation in Europe – you would determine the cost, and save some of your pay each month until you had enough. You would have in fact created for yourself a financial plan in that you (a) determined your goal, and (b) created a plan to achieve it. If you had some money to invest, you would have enlisted the help of a stock broker to assist you in choosing appropriate investments. And if you were concerned about the welfare of your family should something happen to you, you would call on an insurance agent to help you select the appropriate type and amount of insurance. Each of these things, done in isolation from the other, was relatively simple to address.

In the mid-eighties a development occurred that would change the financial services industry dramatically: the personal computer. Financial planning is after all largely about crunching numbers, and nothing beats a computer when it comes to numbers. Prior to the widespread use of computers, projections regarding future financial needs were done by hand with the help of simple calculators. Multiple projections using many different assumptions and taking into account many different variables, while possible, would be tedious and time consuming. Thus, for many years, "financial planning" as an industry would be afforded only by those wealthy enough to pay someone for the considerable time that would be required to perform these calculations.

By the eighties, this was beginning to change. The computer, once regarded as the invention to usher in the paperless world, suddenly began spitting out sheets of paper in quantities previously unimaginable. Among those sheets were financial projections, what-if-scenarios that painted pictures of our financial future, a future that was increasingly broader and more complex.

We have come to realize that financial planning tools can help us resolve the growing tug of war between the various aspects of our financial lives that persisently call upon our resources. Should I save for retirement or for my children's education? Should I buy permanent life insurance or invest in the stock market? These and countless other questions can now be examined with the long-term consequences clearly drawn out in easy-to-understand graphs and charts. Whatever future we long for, a financial plan can guide us towards it, and so it has become the ultimate treasure map.

THE IMPORTANCE OF PLANNING?

Financial planning is not nearly as important as the financial planning industry would like you to think.

When I was a newly appointed General Manager at one of Canada's leading insurers, I was required of course to create a plan, in this case a five year plan for growth and profitability. I spent many hours, days in fact, developing this plan, eager to show the Vice-President that I was deserving of the position he had appointed me to. When the day arrived for me to meet with him to review the plan I was quite excited, proud of the plan I had put together and sure that it would garner his praise. I pushed his copy of the document across the table to him and opened mine to the first page. He quickly took his copy and put it in his brief case. I asked him if we weren't going to review the plan together. His answer was "No, it's really not important what the plan says. What's important is that you have one." That was it. That was the sum total of our discussion and as far as I know, he never looked at the plan at all.

Adding to the allure of financial planning is the tremendous impact of demographics and the needs and wants of our aging boomer population. Life expectancy has rapidly expanded, as has our expectation for leisure at the end of our working careers, making retirement planning an almost universal issue for the first time in history. Higher education has increased both in cost and importance. The number of ways to invest has been increasing exponentially as has the number of ways to spend money. How can we keep track of all of this, and how can we possibly know if we are making the right choices? Financial planning would appear to be the answer to that question.

And so today the *idea* of financial planning is prevalent. Advisors from all of the previous sectors of financial services – insurance, securities, and banking – are busy taking the appropriate courses that will lead to the appropriate designation, which appears to be the Certified Financial Planner (CFP) designation. But the *reality* of financial planning is still evolving.

Most financial plans are assembled by a commissioned sales person who is getting paid for something else. The financial services industry has a long history of charging a fee for delivering a product, be that an investment, an insurance policy or a bank account. For the moment, those fees are sufficient for most planners to be able to provide a "financial plan" as part of the package at little or no cost. Perhaps that's a good thing. Certainly there are many who believe it is not.

Fees are a delicate and emotional issue. But the issue shouldn't be about *price*. The issue should be about *value*. And this is where the disjointed history of financial planning has lead us into a quagmire. What is a financial plan worth? When financial planning as a profession began to take hold it was, as said earlier, reserved for the affluent. Primarily used by executives and professionals, a comprehensive financial plan would cost $3,000 or more. Today, some advisors are providing plans that arguably are superior, at no up front cost. Many would argue that paying $3,000 for objective advice is better value than paying nothing for advice that may be a prelude to a sales pitch.

So the questions continue: Who is a financial planner? What fees are appropriate? How should fees be collected? How do you get objective advice? What issues are covered in a financial plan? Where does financial planning fit into the work done by investment advisors, insurance agents, accountants, tax experts, and so on? If I'm working with a "financial planner," how do I know if I am in fact getting a financial plan?

But there's a more important question, and it is this:

what should a financial plan **do** for me?

If it is truly value we are looking for, that's the question we need to answer.

The Simple Lesson - the essence of financial planning

A new client referred to me recently brought in a financial plan that was prepared by another firm. His company had paid for this service as a part of his benefits package. He pushed the binder across the table and said to me "Here, you may find this useful. It's all Greek to me." I took a quick look at the material, and was reasonably impressed. Wondering what I might be able to add to the work already done I asked, "This seems to be a pretty good plan, what are you hoping I will be able to do for you?" He sighed, indicating some frustration at having to admit that he still needed help and responded, "I'm hoping you can make this stuff simple enough so that even I can understand it. I really just want to know what I should be doing, and why. This plan is overwhelming."

His plea for help illustrates the point that a financial plan is meaningless if it doesn't actually *do* something for you.

Whether your plan is a deluxe leather bound volume of copious pages, or scribbled on the back of a napkin at lunch, it needs to do six distinct things if it is going to be effective. Here they are:

1. Establish or clarify your goals
2. Determine your present situation
3. Map the possible route(s) to your goals
4. Convince you that your goals are achievable
5. Simplify
6. Inspire

Let's look at each one.

Establish or clarify your goals

This of course is the essence of Chapter 2. Without a specific destination in mind, a journey of any sort would appear to be nothing more than mindless wandering. What's surprising is how often this step is overlooked by those engaging in the financial planning process – professionals and amateurs alike.

START WITH THE VISION

For many people, financial planning, and especially retirement planning, is seen as a painful exercise that will help them determine when or if they can in fact retire. In this line of thinking, the vision or goal comes after the plan is put together based on projecting current circumstances into the future. Intuitively we know in fact that goals are imagined first, and then plans are established to pursue them. But what if we imagine goals that turn out to be impossible, or at least too fantastic for us to believe we can achieve based on our present situation?

The art of financial planning is in fact an ongoing exercise of give-and-take between these two opposing points of view. What comes first: the vision or the map to get there? It's always best to start with the vision. If no map can be drawn to reach it, change it. Keep in mind however that as you move towards your established goals, things will change. New ways to accomplish the original goal will appear. Keep that goal in mind, always. Nothing is impossible.

It's easy to overlook the importance of specific goals when there appears to be an obvious *universal* goal – the simple pursuit of more money. Paying less tax, obtaining a better rate of return, lowering expenses, properly structuring debt – these are all designed to do the same thing – increase wealth. Do we need another goal?

The answer is an emphatic **yes.**

And the misunderstanding comes from not knowing how goals are set and achieved. Your goals must be unique to you, believed by you, and inspiring to you. And before you can attempt any meaningful planning, you must determine what specific goals you are pursuing.

Common goal number 1: retirement

Most of us want to retire. And for most of us the retirement vision is very much the same. We won't work, at all, except to volunteer our services to a hospital, church, or charity. We will travel the world and visit all the places we have only seen in movies and travel brochures. We will participate actively in our hobbies, such as golf, or sailing. Finally, we will relax. And, for the most part, we can hardly wait, answering the "when" question with something like "Friday would be good."

The concept of retirement itself has a very brief history. Prior to the early part of the 1900s the idea didn't exist, but as North America limped out of the great depression governments initiated a number of changes that would move older workers out of the work force to make room for younger more capable workers who were sidelined due to the shortage of jobs. Social security and pension plans, along with rapidly increasing life spans suddenly made retirement an important life phase.

The generation that grew up in the 40s and 50s assumed of course that pensions would provide the necessary funds for retirement. That was fine when the usual career lasted 20 to 50 years at "the company." Today's transient and increasingly self-employed workforce isn't able to depend on company or even government benefits to satisfy a growing appetite for expensive leisure activities. Hence retirement planning finds itself front and centre of the baby boomer's long term planning objectives. But there's more.

Today's generation isn't content to work now and play later. They want to work now and play now. And so retirement planning has shifted its focus from accumulating in order to spend later, to answering the question, how can I have what I want while I'm working and even more of what I want when I'm not? In fact, I find that increasingly we are content to consider working longer in order to have it all and have it now.

This discussion only illuminates one aspect of the much larger issue here: retirement is far from a clearly-defined universal idea. It means different things to different people and its importance level ranges from highest to lowest. You need to decide what it means to you. And you need to decide how important it's going to rank in the list of goals you will have for your future.

Common goal number 2: the best life

We want to live the best life we can. This may be obvious, but it begs the question, "what is the best life?" to which there are, no doubt, countless answers. The only answer that matters here is **yours.**

For most, the best life involves the most money. It is money that buys the house, the car, the vacation, and the lifestyle. And it's money that provides us with the sense of freedom that comes with choosing what you want, instead of taking what you can get.

At the risk of moving into philosophical dark waters, let me just say that the pursuit of material possessions can be fraught with disappointment. Like drinking salt water, getting more means wanting more – there is no way to quench this thirst. The important thing to do is to choose carefully and to prioritize the material possessions along with those things that are less tangible.

Here is a simple yet powerful exercise that may assist you in this area. Start a list of all the things you would like to have, and another list of all the things you would like to do. Be as specific as you can. On the list of haves for example you may include: a Porsche, a new kitchen with granite countertops and stainless steel appliances, a 4-bedroom cottage on Lake Joseph, and a Callaway Big Bertha driver. On the list of things you would like to do you may include: travel to Australia, perform in a local theatre company production, write a book, read everything written by Charles Dickens. In the "have" category, you will find almost everything will depend on money, whereas in the latter, you may find many of the things involve no money at all.

MAKING YOUR PLAN COMPREHENSIVE

Comprehensive Financial Planning. Just add the word comprehensive and suddenly it sounds so complicated. Really, it's just the individual pieces, looked at as a whole. If you are doing this yourself, start by examining each component on its own. Plan your retirement, then your children's education, examine your insurance needs, and so on with each aspect of your financial life that should be included. Now, do any of these overlap or conflict? Establish priorities to deal with this. For example, you may decide that your children's education is priority number one. Revise your other plans to allow for this. You are now building a comprehensive financial plan.

Work on these lists over the span of the next few weeks, and continue to revise them – for the rest of your life. Most importantly, prioritize your list. Is the Porsche more important than the cottage, or the trip to Australia? Are any of these more important than those things you hope to pursue in retirement? There are no rights or wrongs in this exercise. Just be sure that those items of highest priority are incorporated into your financial plan.

Common goal number 3: provide for your children

We want to ensure our children are given every opportunity to excel by giving them the best education possible and the funds they may need to begin life in an expensive world. Nothing is more important.

And yet for many people, the financial costs of everyday living, and the irresistible pursuit of happiness in the here and now, often make it difficult to apply financial resources to such distant needs as university tuition 15 years from now. For others, this priority becomes so all consuming that all other goals are held hostage.

As always, the best solution is somewhere in between. While it's important to prepare for what might appear to be an obvious and important expense, it's also important to remember that somehow our generation managed to become educated without the benefit of RESPs and the like. The key is to find the proper perspective and to understand that looking after one's own financial future is every bit as important to your children as looking after theirs.

Common goal number 4: financial independence

We want to be financially independent as long as we live. This goal isn't always discussed – it really doesn't need to be. It is an implied objective of any financial plan. We simply don't want to outlive our money.

There are many questions to think about when attempting to quantify this particular goal. How long will you live? How much will it cost to live that far into the future? What kind of investment returns will you achieve between now and

THE POWER OF PROFESSIONAL HELP

If you are looking to create a comprehensive financial plan, one that encompasses retirement planning, estate planning, cash management, and risk management, then it would be foolish to suggest that anything other than professional help is the way to go. This kind of planning, even with the aid of today's sophisticated planning software, is anything but simple. That said, the output, the part that you will see, should most certainly be simple. You should understand it, and it should inspire you to take action towards accomplishing the many goals it will be designed to pursue. If it doesn't, find another planner.

the end, and will you need to become increasingly conservative (meaning accepting lower and lower investment returns) as you get older? How will healthcare expenses change and if you needed personal care, how much will that cost?

None of these questions have definitive answers, but all of them may be handled by making some reasonable assumptions.

So, as you begin the exercise of building a financial plan, you first lay down, in order, the list of goals you hope to achieve, both in the short term and the long term. If these aren't clear, there is little hope that your financial plan will provide you with anything useful.

Determine your present situation

If you were dropped into the middle of a busy city and wanted to find your way home, what's the first thing you would try to find out? Of course you would want to know where you are, even if possible down to the exact street location. The point is, before you take the first step, you must know where you are now. With respect to financial planning this is simply a matter of taking stock of present resources. How much do you presently have? How much do you owe? How much are you earning? How much are you spending? Exactly where are you financially?

For many people this is a truly enlightening exercise. It is very common today to have accounts with several banks, investments with several advisors or institutions, and multiple debts of varying duration. With things so scattered, surprisingly few can accurately answer the question, "What is your net worth?"

But this is critical. You will find a template for creating your own statement of net worth in the Appendix, or on our website at **www.bellfinancial.ca**. Fill it in, or see a financial planner. You can't take the next step without knowing two things: where you want to go, and where you are now.

Map the possible route(s) to the goals

This is the most obvious objective of a financial plan. It is also by far the most complex, and arguably the least important. Allow me to explain.

A financial plan should by definition outline steps to be taken in order to accomplish the various goals. Much like a road map, the bends in the road and the points at which you must leave one highway and turn onto another should be clearly marked. The only problem is with your financial plan, the destination is constantly changing, and the routes are in a constant state of flux. If you have ever tried to find an address in a new neighbourhood on an old map, you have some idea of what I mean.

It would be simplest of course to go between two points on a map "as the crow flies." In other words, draw a straight line. But maps aren't like that. And neither is life.

Consider for example the goal of saving for retirement. To keep this example simple, let's suppose that you have determined that you want to have $1 million in investment assets by the time you retire, in 20 years. You have further assumed that you will invest your accumulating savings at an average rate of 6%, and your balance at the moment is zero. Let's assume zero taxation, meaning that all of the savings are in a registered plan. Using a financial calculator it's easy to determine that you should be saving $2,195 per month. Your next steps are clear. Open the investment account, and deposit $2,195. Repeat the deposit each month for the next 240 months. The result should be $1 million.

There are many problems with this approach. First of all, most people find the steps required today are too big. If you are saving nothing now, and suddenly need to save $2,195 per month to reach your goals, you may quickly deduce that your goals are too lofty. Also, most people would quickly realize that it would be smarter to assume that savings will increase as income increases. So the question might be, what do I need to save each month this year, increased at 3% each year thereafter? (3% is my assumption for inflation.) The answer is $1,729 per month. (That's this year. In the last of our 20 years the monthly savings will be $3,122.) For most, this solution will still be too high.

The workable solution will start to emerge when we look more closely at the map, and ask ourselves, what changes lay ahead that are going to dramatically change the speed at which I can travel? When will I be on the "expressway" to retirement savings? Most people have a number of opportunities to accelerate savings, most commonly when debts are retired, and when children graduate from school.

Perhaps you have a mortgage that will be paid off many years prior to retirement. Once the debt is retired you could direct your mortgage payments into retirement savings. We may also want to re-examine the goal itself. How did we choose $1 million? Is it too high? And if it isn't, there still may be opportunities to plan around expenses associated with children including the savings needed for education, or dramatic changes in career that may cause higher increases in income.

Some may be reluctant to consider these kinds of things part of a good strategy. More than once I have heard someone say, "How can you be so sure that things will be better in the future, allowing me to save more?" The answer of course is "I can't." But, ask yourself this to put this into focus. Think back 10 or 20 years. Could you have predicted you would be where you are today? Are things better or worse than you would have predicted? I'm not suggesting you count on luck,

MEET SHARON AND BRIAN WALKER

Not everyone needs a financial planner. Sharon Walker is a member of a defined contribution pension plan that we manage, and she asked me to meet with her to review her investment selections. After asking her a few questions, I suggested that perhaps I should meet with both her and her husband and put together a comprehensive financial plan. She somewhat reluctantly agreed. Sharon and her husband Brian had a very specific, and very simple plan. They would use all available resources to pay down their mortgage, which was their only debt. Once the debt was retired they would then apply all available resources to saving for retirement. Based on this plan they had virtually zero in RRSPs. The only saving they had done was through Sharon's defined contribution pension plan, which was of course not optional. Brian had a non-contributory defined benefit pension plan.

They weren't in a particular hurry to retire, but Brian had done some rough calculations and based on pensions, government benefits, and their own savings, he had estimated that they would be in a position to retire by his age 60.

My sophisticated financial planning software proved Brian to be right. In fact, they could probably retire a year sooner. But of course I was also able to show that by contributing to their RRSPs now, instead of waiting, while the debt would drag on a little longer, they would be substantially further ahead overall. In fact, they could easily retire at Brian's age 55 if they followed my recommendations.

Brian and Sharon listened politely to my overview of the financial plan, but I could tell they were not engaged. They had a plan and were following that plan, a plan that I had reinforced. For both of them, retiring sooner wasn't as important as getting out of debt sooner. The thought of being debt-free was their source of inspiration.

As I drove away from the meeting I realized just how simple this whole thing can be. Their plan could easily be put together without the use of any financial planning tools at all. And it would work for virtually anyone. As usual, the simple plan was the better plan.

TOOLS FOR FINANCIAL PLANNING

Tools for the financial planning journey are abundantly available for those wishing to journey without a guide. You can find many of these at a number of websites, including our own: **www.bellfinancial.ca** My best advice to the do-it-yourselfer is this: most of the time, the mathematical modeling you do on your own is going to make the journey appear more difficult than it really is. Examine your own history for proof of that. Don't let false obstacles push you into making unrealistic assumptions, or worse, taking uncomfortable risks. Set your sights on your goals, and move forward with determination and belief. There are many things in your future, things you can't imagine at the moment, which are going to "push" you forward. You simply need to make sure you are moving in the right direction when the push is received.

nor am I looking for some flimsy excuse to procrastinate. But a healthy dose of optimism is valuable, perhaps even essential to live an extraordinary life.

Convince yourself that your goals are achievable

In the end, I believe this is what financial planning is all about.

Think about a time that you found something you really wanted (and ended up getting), but hesitated because it was outside what you believed you could afford. It might have been a car, an article of clothing, a house, or a variety of things. How did you end up changing your mind?

Likely you went through a mental exercise best described as rationalization. Perhaps you found some way to justify the indulgence – some way to argue it would be good for you. Or perhaps you realized that you could simply cut an expense elsewhere and in fact you could afford it, if you decided it was a priority. Perhaps you stretched out the financing to lower the payments and make it seem more affordable. Whatever you did, in the end, you changed what you believed. You starting out believing it might ruin you financially to make the decision. Then you convinced yourself that this belief was wrong, in fact you could handle this expense. You convinced yourself that your goal was achievable.

You wouldn't have proceeded without changing your belief. Henry Ford said it best; "Whether you think you can or you think you can't, you're right." Life of course is lived somewhere in between, with doubts and uncertainty, hopes and dreams. The goal of financial planning is to move you closer to the realm of belief, the realm of certain success.

Your financial plan should take your various goals and by showing you exactly how they can be accomplished in turn say to you "see, these things are achievable." Believe. Move forward with your plans.

Simplify

Another important goal of financial planning (and most certainly of this book), is that of simplifying. This may seem like a tall order. Our financial system, which includes an endless array of investment choices, financing strategies, and tax laws may appear to make simplification impossible.

But the truth is, the accumulation of wealth is very much about the simple but steady application of habits. We need to create a plan that distills this truth into a series of steps that we can not only understand, but follow repeatedly over the course of many years.

Let's go back to the example of being dropped into the middle of a busy city. Try to imagine how you would feel. Imagine the city was foreign; all the signs and the voices around you were in a language you didn't speak and didn't even recognize. Your initial feelings would most likely be fear. Fear of the unknown. Fear is in fact a surprisingly common feeling when it comes to financial matters for many people, and it's a very similar fear – fear of the unknown.

But when it comes to financial matters you actually have all sorts of information at your fingertips to quickly pinpoint your exact location and determine precisely the direction you should head to find your way to the airport, all written in a language you understand. Financial planning should eliminate those fears. Creating a complicated plan only exacerbates them.

MEET TIA AND JEREMY FONTANA

Tia and Jeremy Fontana felt as thought their lives were racing out of control. Jeremy is a self-employee consultant, and Tia works for a major bank. But their combined income of $150,000 still didn't seem to be enough to pay the mortgage, household expenses and the added costs of daycare for their two small children. Tia wondered if it was time to consider leaving the workforce which probably mean moving to a less expensive house, so that she could stay home with the kids and they all could slow down their hectic lives.

Despite their belief to the contrary, they had actually done a pretty good job of saving so far. The problem was they had 7 different RRSP accounts, and since none were of any great size, they had convinced themselves that their savings were small. They had also started an RESP, and their mortgage was well under control with plenty of equity in the home.

When we initially looked at the financial plan I created for them, they kept looking at the balance sheet as if it belonged to someone else. More than once, each of them said, "We're worth that much?" In terms of basic financial planning, they truly didn't know where they were starting from, until now.

We looked at a couple of different long range projections, one showing Tia remaining in the workforce and another with her staying home for the next 4 years. A dialogue ensued that was decidedly differ

Inspire

When the planning process is over, you should be experiencing a sense of excitement. You have laid down plans to accomplish some of your most important goals. You have worked through the ways to accomplish those goals, and convinced yourself that they are achievable. Furthermore, you know what needs to be done, and are able to take the next step. Sounds to me like a recipe for inspiration.

Belief and inspiration may both be unusual ingredients in a recipe for something as left-brain as financial planning, but without them, the exercise is nothing more than the production of charts and graphs.

ent than the discussion we had had in the first meeting. Initially Tia especially was feeling a need to release pressure, somehow. Now she was carefully considering two very valid options.

In the end, Tia decided to stay at work, but for the right reason. She loved her job and needed the balance it provided in her life. The pressure they had been experiencing regarding financial matters was greatly alleviated, and they started planning things that they could do as opposed to discussing things they believed they had to do to survive. In truth, very little change took place in how their dollars were spent or saved. We did consolidate their investments, but mostly we just organized their thoughts. We determined their starting point, and set a course for some specific goals. Suddenly, a life previously careening out of control became the extraordinary life they had been wishing for.

I knew that the financial plan had been inspiring, but the proof came a few weeks later. Julie, a friend of the Fontanas, called in and said that she and her husband had seen them at a party on the weekend. She was clearly energized when she said to me, "Tia and Jeremy are so excited about the work you did with them, and well, Nick and I, we want some of that." "That" of course, was inspiration.

After the planning process is complete you should have clarity about your highest priority goals. This alone should ensure that you are feeling inspired. But you also have clarity about your present financial position, and perhaps for the first time, you aren't feeling that you are lost in a foreign city of financial products and services. By simplifying your financial picture and creating simple steps to move you toward your goal, you now truly know where you are and where you are going. The financial plan has proven to you that your goals are achievable and so armed with the conviction that only belief can build, you take that first step with confidence.

That's inspiration. Your financial affairs are now simple. The life you are heading directly towards is **extraordinary.**

SIMPLE MONEY	EXTRAORDINARY LIFE
Create simple financial models to show how you can realize your goals.	List and prioritize all of your goals.
Determine where, exactly, you are right now. Complete a net worth statement.	Let your goals flow from the vision of your ideal future.
	Planning is a belief-building exercise. Prove to yourself that your goals can be realized.
Keep it simple. If you don't understand a plan, it's of no value.	How do you know if a financial plan is going to work? By how inspired you are to take action because of it.

Cash **management**

If you dream of finding peace in your financial life, this is the way. The only way.

A brief historical perspective

Money is as old as recorded history. But for most of that history wealth was measured in terms of hard assets. Land and real estate, jewels, and of course precious metals that were minted into monetary coins – money. And for much of history the acquiring and accumulating of wealth, especially money, was no easy task. Inheriting it was the best way. Stealing and swindling worked, although generally frowned upon. But slowly accumulating wealth by "working" for someone else just wasn't an option.

Paper money, easy access to credit, and electronic transactions have changed all that. We are the most affluent society ever to live on the planet. We have access to our cash at all times, and can transmit it anywhere in the world at the push of a button. We can borrow – in fact we are strongly encouraged to borrow, to finance almost anything.

Much has changed in how we view and manage money, and much of that change has taken place a just the past few decades. Consider the changes from one generation to the next. When my parents were first married and raising five children back in the 50's and 60's, they had exactly two places from which to get funds. The cash they received on pay day, and the money they had on deposit at the bank. Spending beyond their means wasn't an option. They would simply run out. When my parents decided to buy a piece of land and build their own home, they couldn't get a bank loan. So they went to a friend of means and asked for a loan. The friend agreed and gave them 100% of the funds necessary to get the house built and fit to live in. My parents faithfully repaid that loan, in cash, for fifteen years, not refinancing once. My mother finally moved out of that house in the year 2000 – 48 years after it was built.

It's a different story today. We now can access our money via debit card, several credit cards, cheques, on-line transfers, bank machines on most corners, a line of credit, instant loans, and perhaps even the cash in our pockets. We can get money and spend money literally in the blink of an eye.

Speed perhaps is our greatest danger. We are in a **hurry.** We don't want to wait until tomorrow. Life is blazing past and our fear of being left behind is overwhelming. So we spend the money we have today. And we spend tomorrow's money – today. Things are moving so fast that in terms of spending we are actually days, months, perhaps even years ahead of ourselves.

Not surprisingly, we long for things to slow down. We reminisce about the days when things were simpler. In days gone by it wasn't this hard to stay afloat. No one got stuck perpetually in the fast lane of our consumer driven society. There were checks and balances in place to ensure that life tomorrow would be very much like life today. We didn't manage our money. We managed our lives.

Today, unlike the generations before us, we need to manage our money for fear o careening out of control. But here's the good news: there's a very simple lesson tha we can learn from our parents (who learned it from their parents). It's quite simple to understand, and it never fails when applied. Here it is.

The simple lesson

Spend less than you make.

That's it. In the pages to follow I'll elaborate on this simple point, but really, that's all that needs to be said. In fact, your financial success hinges entirely on this simple lesson. So let's say it again, more loudly.

Spend **less** than you make.

Applying the lesson for an extraordinary life

Let me guess: you're disappointed. We all would love to find the secret to wealth that would allow us to defy this simple lesson. God knows we have tried a lot of different things. Mortgages, bank loans, lines of credit, credit cards, gambling, just to name a few. They may even appear to work for a short time. But ultimately, logic prevails. Spending $10 while earning $9 is a recipe for disaster.

There are countless books, workshops, and videos that propose to teach you how to manage your money. They will range from those that want to help you find contentment in spending less than you do now, to those that lead you to hope that making money is simply a matter of getting on the right train, and when the cash starts rolling in all of your problems will disappear. Most of these are hype. Most miss the point altogether. And most in fact take you in precisely the wrong direction.

The truth is, we need to think *less* about money. Most hyped-up strategies suggest you can solve money problems by making more, or by figuring out how to get a loaf of bread for 10% less. But these cause you even more stress by forcing you to think about money more and more.

But here's the real problem with most of these strategies. They lead you to believe that the answer is "out there." The voice in our head keeps saying "there must be some tip, some strategy, some understanding that will lead me to the right path on spending, earning and saving for the future." This leads to a mountain of "excuses" that cause us to overlook the simple truth and lay the blame for our

MEET MARY BROWN

One of the most surprising things about being a financial planner is the gradual realization that statistics tell us very little about real people. The average person might spend $x on housing, and have $y dollars in their RRSP, but the average person in fact, doesn't exist. Some people in fact are very far from the average.

One such person is Mary Brown.

Mary Brown lives in downtown Toronto. She lives in a small house with her father. She doesn't live with Dad to decrease her financial burden but rather, Dad lives with her to reduce his. It's Mary's income that pays the majority of the bills.

Many financial experts suggest that living in Toronto requires a family income of at least $80,000. Mary's income is $30,000. But Mary shows no sign of struggling under any financial burden. In fact, when we meet for her annual review, she spends much of her time trying to determine how she might increase the amount she gives away. She says things like "Do you think it would be ok if I put aside $25 per month to save for my niece's education?" She is keenly aware of how much excess she has each month. And she has faithfully contributed her maximum RRSP allowance each year.

In terms of equipping herself to live in the same lifestyle during retirement, Mary is well ahead of most, not just because she has saved so much, but because she needs so little. If things stay as they are,

increasing debt and constant stress on someone else's shoulders. Consider the following examples:

"We didn't have much when I was a child, and I was determined not to let my children live without. I buy them nice things, we live in a big home, and we take expensive vacations so they will have a better childhood than I did." **It's the parents' fault.**

"We want to live for today. We don't know if we'll be here in 20 years, or even tomorrow. We wanted a pool now, so we can enjoy it today." **It's the neighbours' fault -** they already have a pool, and it looked like a lot of fun.

Mary could retire comfortably in 10 years, at the age of 49. The funny thing is, I know she won't stop working at that point. She'll end up instead being far wealthier than she can imagine.

When I first met Mary I left the meeting feeling somewhat ashamed of myself. In a very real sense, Mary was in much better shape financially than I was, even though my income and account balances might suggest otherwise. And Mary appeared to be completely without financial stress, something I am quite unaccustomed to seeing in anyone, let alone someone living on a fraction of the income most of us enjoy. I wondered perhaps if I was living my life the right way!

The lesson from Mary is that we can all find happiness when we live our lives in alignment with our values. Mary focuses much of her energy and her time on those things most important to her, her family and her church, so that she has no need to find other things to fill her time or her life. And she is so certain that keeping her financial house in order is an important component of living that she does it naturally and without regret for the things she might be missing out on. Her beliefs, and her habits, are perfectly in sync.

Mary also stands out in my mind as the living proof that happiness isn't linked to absolute levels of wealth. Very few people would place Mary among the wealthy. To Mary, money is remarkably simple. But her life, by all important measures, is extraordinary.

"I deserve more money than I'm making. I'm not recognized at work for what I contribute. I have a hard time living on my current income." **It's the boss's fault.**

"How can you live here and not want to drive a nice car, live in a nice house, and have nice things?" Good point. **It's society's fault.**

Let's get one thing straight: there is no one to blame but **you.** You are the master of your own destiny. You make the choices. You will be living with the consequences. You. As soon as you get that, as soon as you take responsibility for your financial life and accept the fact that you have, right now, all the power you need to create the perfect life, the sooner you will arrive at that place you've been seeking.

This is the only area with respect to money in which you are actually in control. Think about it: how much time and energy is devoted to teaching you about things like investing, inflation, taxes and borrowing? Yet, how much control do you or anyone else for that matter have over the rates of return you earn on investments, inflation, taxes, and lending rates? If we are honest, we have to say zero. It is perhaps a great irony that we spend most of our time trying to control the things that are uncontrollable, and almost no time managing the one thing that we alone affect!

How we handle our money is a **habit.** That's why someone who changes jobs or careers and finds themselves with substantially more money still finds themselves living beyond their means. That's why someone who wins the lottery and quits his job, finds himself back at work within a few years. It's not that we are in the habit of spending a certain amount of money or having a certain lifestyle, it's that we are in the habit of being stretched financially. We have a vision of ourselves as people who have a hard time making ends meet. Our habits are a direct result of the vision we hold of who we are. Our beliefs about ourselves and our place in the world are by far our most limiting characteristic.

We don't lack discipline. We are perfectly disciplined to our current habits. We need a different set of habits. We need to see ourselves in a different way.

A NEW MEASURE OF HAPPINESS

Newsflash: money and happiness aren't linked. In his new book, *A Whole New Mind,* author Daniel Pink suggests that the U.S. needs a new barometer for measuring prosperity – "Gross National Happiness." According to Pink, research done by psychologists, neuroscientists, and behavioral economists points to an undeniable truth: more money doesn't make us much happier. Far more important are things like relationships, engaging work, meaning and purpose in life. Worth thinking about.

CASH MANAGEMENT

If you have money woes related to spending and saving, then you see yourself as someone with money woes related to spending and saving. You probably think this is your "lot" in life. Destiny has cursed you with this burden. That's not true. You can change all that in a heartbeat. How, you ask? Here are a few tips that may help point you in the right direction.

1. Stop looking for answers "out there"

So long as you believe that someone else can help with this, you will not attempt to do the work yourself. As Steven Covey says, "If you think the problem is out there, stop. That is the problem." I can't offer any better advice than this. Accept your money troubles as *your* problem, and your problem is over.

2. Know thyself

The Greeks believed this was the secret to success. They may have been right. What do you need to know about yourself with respect to cash management? Simple. *How do you spend your money now?*

Surprisingly few people know. Here's a typical conversation.

"How much do you spend each month?"

"All of it."

"Where does the money go?"

"I have no idea."

You might as well be trying to figure out what happens to **socks** when they disappear in the **laundry.**

THE TALE OF THE APPLE FARMERS

Once upon a time there were two brothers, Bob and Joe. They bought an apple orchard and set out to run a successful business. After the first few months of their first fall apple picking season, they realized that things weren't going too well. Their financial picture seemed to be getting darker, and so they did what many astute business people do, they hired a consultant. The consultant spent the next several weeks studying every facet of their enterprise. Finally, he met with the brothers to deliver his findings.

He pointed out that the total cost of producing a bushel of apples was approximately $10. Each morning the brothers loaded their truck to capacity and took them to the farmer's market, where they sold them for $9 per bushel. The consultant smiled as he delivered his succinct recommendation. The brothers needed a bigger truck.

It's a mystery. And this leads to a firm belief that managing money is an impossible task. It's not. Start by simply analyzing where your money is going by tracking it over several months. Use your cheque books, bank and credit card statements, and whatever other information you have to piece together a picture of your current spending. What you are unable to find evidence of, or track, label miscellaneous. Your goal in this exercise is to make the miscellaneous category as small as possible. Use the "Current Cash Flow Statement" that you can find at **www.bellfinancial.ca** to guide you. Add categories as needed to make it yours.

3. Create a spending plan

Notice how I have avoided the word "budget?" The fact is, for most of us, that's a nasty word. It implies restrictions, sacrifice, lack of choice, compromise. We want freedom.

Accepting that you cannot have everything you want right now isn't the same as accepting that you can never have it. And that's the key to making this whole spending-cash-flow thing (still avoiding the word budget) work. Have it all by having a plan.

CASH MANAGEMENT

Armed with the information from your "Current Cash Flow Statement," make changes to your cash flow projections to form your "Spending Plan." It's a plan, not a binding contract, and I guarantee you will not spend exactly according to your plan. But you may find yourself making some different choices. You may find that in some areas, your spending changes. Then you will be moving in the right direction.

Check this plan periodically against your actual spending. Make changes to either your actual spending, or your spending plan so that eventually the two line up. You may think you need someone else to help you "get on track." You don't. You just need to stop keeping this information from the only person who really can help you: **yourself.**

4. Look at the total costs of items purchased on credit

Credit cards, consumer loans, and no-money-down-pay-nothing-until-2099 plans create an illusion. They don't make things more affordable. They make them more expensive. Buy a car and finance the entire thing and you turn a $35,000 purchase into a $772.95 per month payment. (Payment assumes a 60 month loan at 6% and 15% in total taxes). This works, because we don't have the lump sum in the bank but convince ourselves that we can carry the monthly payment. But the truth is, that $35,000 vehicle will end up taking $46,377 out of your pocket. (60 payments of $772.95).

And the $500 leather coat (that was marked down from $600 and so can't be resisted) that is purchased on a credit card with an 18% interest rate and then carried on that card for the next 12 months actually will cost $678.50 by the end of the year. And if you don't pay it off then, the price will keep rising.

The real kicker on the buy-now-and-pay-later plan is that often, by the time we get to the point at which we finish paying for the thing we bought, it no longer appears that valuable to us! The debt is now an unfortunate burden. This actually encourages us to make "minimum" payments only, and thus makes a bad situation worse.

The **lesson** here is this: look at the all-in costs when you make a purchase, and set out a specific plan to pay the price. Even if the financing is the "no money down and no interest ever" type of plan, stop for a second and ask yourself, can I afford to pay cash for this now? If not, what makes you think you will be able to when the time comes to pay up?

5. Focus on changing behaviour

Spending money is a habit. Accept this simple fact and you can get down to the business of actually changing your behaviour. If you want to experience abundance, you need to alter your behaviour to allow you to spend less than you are making, and include in your spending plan appropriate allocations to giving and saving.

ARE YOU AN "AVERAGE" SAVER?

In case you need "empirical data" to back up the obvious, Statistics Canada suggests that the amount of money Canadians save each year, as a percentage of income, has been in steady decline for more than 20 years. In the early 80s the savings rate in Canada was 15%. That is, on average, Canadians were saving 15% of their income. By the early 90s that had fallen to 9%, and by 2001 to 5%. In the early stages of 2004 it was reported at 1.5%. Zero isn't too far off.

The danger in these kinds of numbers is that it can seduce you, once again, into thinking that it's not your fault. Some great North American conspiracy – consumerism - is preventing you from saving. It's not just you. Everybody's in the same boat. It can't be helped.

Slap yourself. These are statistics, based on averages. Are you average? Is that your goal? Remember, you have full control over your spending. I have yet to find a single client who hasn't been able to find a way to change spending habits to fit into long term plans. Not all have done it. But none have lacked the ability.

Start small.

Experts in this area agree that it takes at least 21 days to change a pattern of behaviour. Try it out on something of lesser significance. For example, if you spend $10 per week buying lottery tickets, for the next three weeks (21 days) spend only $5 per week. Then try $0 per week.

Then try something more meaningful. For example, you may have noticed that you spend far more than you expected on clothing. If that's the case, chances are you shop on a regular basis. And you use a credit card. So try this for the next month (ok, slightly longer than 21 days). Resolve that on the next credit card statement, your allotment to clothing will be zero. That's right, zero. Make all of your clothing purchases with cash. No, you don't get points for using cash like you do when you use the credit card. But you may get something else: richer.

This kind of change may appear painful, but it will force you to address habits, (or addictions) that you have been ignoring. If all fails in this little example, then revisit your spending plan and increase your allocation to clothing to what you are actually going to spend. But be sure to take those dollars from something else. You can ignore the truth, but it's still there, and you are not in control. Face it and deal with it, and suddenly you are back in the driver's seat.

6. Save/invest a portion of your income each month

If your spending plan does not include a monthly allocation to your RRSP or some other savings or investment vehicle, revise it. This strategy is supported in almost every book on this subject and comes under a lot of different headings. "Pay yourself first" for example. It is also a remarkably astute investment strategy best known as dollar cost averaging (to be covered again in a later chapter). But the biggest advantage it will have for you is developing a habit. A habit that will actually get you to your destination.

If it appears to you that currently your spending plan is already too stretched, then think smaller. It doesn't matter if it's $25 or $2,500 each month, find a number you can live with and start putting it away. Gradually increase it, and like other

WHAT SHOULD YOU BE DOING WITH YOUR LIFE?

From a distance, it's easy to admire and envy people who have a lot of money. They live in fantastic houses, drive fabulous cars, get invited to all the great parties, and truly live the life of "the rich and famous." But check your experience regarding the people you actually know and you will no doubt find that those people who truly light up the room and capture your admiration have something else in common. They love what they do.

Po Bronson, author of *What Should I Do With My Life?: The True Story of People Who Answered the Ultimate Question*, writes, "Those who are lit by that passion are the object of envy among their peers and the subject of intense curiosity. They are the source of good ideas. They make the extra effort. They demonstrate the commitment. They are the ones who, day by day, will rescue this drifting ship. And they will be rewarded. With money, sure, and responsibility, undoubtedly. But with something even better too: the kind of satisfaction that comes with knowing your place in the world." Think about it. What should you be doing with *your* life?

goals, set a target amount that you hope to reach by some point in the future. The important thing is to develop the habit, and see the kind of progress you can make with steady contributions. Eventually this will take priority over other items currently on your budget, and then you really will be making **progress.**

7. Love your work, or find work that you love

Wait a minute. What does this have to do with cash management? Well, spending is only half the equation. Making the money is the other half. And if you are looking to lead an extraordinary life, however you define it, your working life figures into it.

Please don't take this as advice to quit your job and start looking for that dream job, unless you happen to know exactly what that is. But I am advising you to start thinking about that dream job. And the place to start is exactly where you are right now. Start by loving your current job.

If you don't love your work, why not? What would need to change in order for you to love it? Does the person (people) responsible for making such changes know about this? Are you silently hoping someone will read your mind? And if your current job is beyond any hope of you actually finding it rewarding, why are you not looking elsewhere? Have you simply resigned yourself to working for a paycheque?

The best hope you have of dramatically increasing your top line, the money coming in, is to love your work. Pay scales, unions, and corporate policies are all aligned to work against you on this. They serve the needs of those who are satisfied to merely be pulled along. If you want to jump out, you need to stand out. And nothing stands out like passion.

Love your **work.** Or find work that you will love. It quite possibly will lead to greater financial rewards. But that is not what is so important about this idea. The fact is if your life is going to be extraordinary, this is an absolute imperative.

8. Properly track expenses paid for on credit

Credit may be the most destructive financial illusion of our time. The point is best illustrated by sharing a recent conversation I had with a new client.

John and I were reviewing his Spending Plan. Under debt repayments, he had listed "credit card payments" and the amount was $800 per month. I asked John for clarification on this. He told me this was the minimum monthly payment, which he was proud to say they faithfully made each month.

"What is the total outstanding balance on those credit cards?" I ask.

"About $25,000."

I made a note to add this to his balance sheet.

"And how much did you actually charge to the credit cards last month?" I query.

"Oh, probably about $1,000 in total," was his casual response.

"So, it's safe to say that your credit card balance is likely to grow."

"Yes, but we are near the limit on most cards, so it can't grow much more," John pointed out.

"And the $1,000 charged to your credit card last month, are those items included in your spending plan elsewhere? For example, if you went out to dinner and charged it to your credit card did that expense fit into your monthly spending plan for dining out?"

"Hmm. Let's see. I think the major expense was the new dishwasher we bought, so no, it's not a real "budget" item." (He used the budget word, not me.)

"That's a potential **problem** then, isn't it?" I point out.

"What do you mean?" he asks, truly looking puzzled.

"Well if someone is spending outside the spending plan, you're going to exceed it, aren't you?"

"Yeah, but it was on credit, so it's not really a monthly expense. I mean, the payment is a monthly expense, and I've included that." I could see John starting to squirm.

Is anyone starting to see, and perhaps even personally relate to, this problem?

"Of the $800 payment you make John, how much of that is interest?"

"Not sure."

Exactly.

Here's the real deal. The interest you pay on your

credit cards, (in John's case about $375 per month), is an expense. It should be included in your monthly expenses, so long as you expect to continue to carry a balance.

Items charged to your credit card each month - every last item - are also expenses. They must show up somewhere in your spending plan. Maybe not as a monthly item – John isn't going to buy a dishwasher every month – but at least as an annual item. Next year it will be a stove, a new roof, or some other item for the home.

Payments made to your credit cards are part interest and part principal, and the principal portion of this can be ignored. It's simply a transfer from one account, your bank, to another account, your credit card. But it has no real effect on your net worth.

9. Think net worth

The lesson from the credit card example leads perfectly to this idea. Think net worth. Measure your net worth frequently. It's the only real measure of your progress. As debts diminish, your net worth climbs. As investments increase, net worth climbs. When measuring the value of one strategy over another, think net worth. This is remarkably valuable when answering one of the more frequently asked questions, "Should I pay down my debt or invest?"

Don't actually know your net worth right now? As stated previously,

"know thyself."

MEET TOM AND MARTHA MARONETTI

When Tom and Martha Maronetti met me for the first time a number of years ago, they were anxious about the fact that they weren't saving as much as they wanted to for retirement. They were also in "panic mode" about their nest egg's decline during the tech market bust of the early 2000's. They wanted guidance in two ways. First, help them shave some additional dollars off their spending, and second, get them into investments that were increasing in value.

My first response was to tell them that I could do neither of these things. But, I added, neither could anyone else. What I could do however was to help them discover what the "real" problem was. They hesitated, but agreed to press on with a financial plan.

The Maronetti's were in fact well on their way to financial independence and if desired, early retirement - Tom from his job as a plant manager, Martha from her job in a local nursery school. They had already saved more than enough for the education of their two sons, who were 14 and 12 at the time. They had made maximum contributions annually to their RRSPs and pensions, and Tom had participated in the company stock purchase plan. They had paid off their mortgage about 2 years prior to our meeting. Since that time, they had allocated the mortgage payment amount to a non-registered investment account that Tom was personally managing along with the RRSP assets.

Tom did not like his job and was counting the days to retirement. Martha loved hers, but was also counting the days for Tom, looking forward to the time when Tom could escape the stress of his work.

10. Live in gratitude

This is the short cut. How we manage our cash is a function of our habits. Our habits are driven by the vision we hold, the beliefs we have, about who we are. And for most of us, that vision is stuck in the present.

The future you - the one you dream about while secretly believing is unattainable - has everything you need and everything you want. Everything. When that point is reached you will no doubt feel an overwhelming emotional response that is best described as gratitude.

CASH MANAGEMENT

In the end, my advice was not what either of them expected. Tom needed to find new work, or stop working so much overtime and find a way to enjoy the work he was doing now. They needed to spend more money. They hadn't had a vacation in over 5 years, and yet our plan showed that an annual family vacation was easily within reach. They could stop contributing to the education funds and the non-registered funds and I suggested they find ways to increase, not decrease, their month to month spending. As for their investments, they simply needed to leave them alone.

I wish I could tell you that they took all the advice and now live the life fantastic. Not quite. But Tom did quit his job. Unfortunately, he took a different job that looks pretty much the same as the job he had before. More pay, yes, but also more demands, and more stress. That is currently under review. The important thing here is that he's looking. He actually said in a recent meeting "I know now that I would rather work until 60 at something I love, than until 55 at something I hate." I noticed Martha smile when he said that. I responded "You might even want to work to 65."

Last winter they took the boys to a resort in Florida. They drove, of course, but by all accounts, they had a great time. They passed the management of their investments off to me. Occasionally I still need to remind them that these go up, and down. They stopped saving so aggressively and the extra is beginning to make them feel much better about the current state of affairs. They go out to dinner and the movies more regularly.

Bit by bit they are letting go of old habits. They are simplifying their relationship with money, and they are steadily moving closer to the life they really want. The extraordinary life they thought could only exist in retirement is perhaps just around the corner.

You might think the feeling you are pursuing is that of accomplishment - the pride of achievement. But this side of you will always find the next challenge and more to want. Always.

No, it's the state of gratitude that will finally usher you into the world of financial peace.

And here's the most remarkable idea I could possibly share with you: you can reach that state right now, right this second. Just be grateful for all that you have.

See your glass not as half empty, not even as half full, but as entirely full. Push out the thoughts of need and want and focus your thoughts on all the wonderful things that are yours. If you are reading this book you have much to be thankful for.

Live in a state of gratitude. If you can do this, the rest of this book is unnecessary for you.

And your life is indeed already **extraordinary.**

SIMPLE MONEY	EXTRAORDINARY LIFE
Spend less time thinking about money.	Spend more time living.
Don't work for money.	Work with passion and for meaning in whatever you do.
Use credit cards – they're convenient.	Pay your credit card balances each month and remain free of their strangling costs.
Stop wanting money. It's not money you want.	Expect the best and give thanks for whatever comes along.
You know all you need to know about money. You. The answers aren't "out there."	Enjoy the ride. You aren't making any mistakes.
Know where you spend your money.	Know where you want to spend your money. Know what you want.
Spend less than you make. Save a little every month.	Accumulate wealth, steadily.
Change your behaviour. Start small.	
Think net worth.	

Chapter 5

Investing

The extraordinary life is not one in which we are financial experts – it's one in which we have all of our needs met, and all of our dreams fulfilled.

A brief historical perspective

As recently as the 1700s, our position in society was predetermined at birth. If we were fortunate enough to be born into the family that *owned* the land, we would enjoy a life of comfort. On the other hand if we were born into one of the families that *worked* the land, we were destined for a life of struggle. There was no such thing as "working hard to get ahead," or indeed, investing well to rise above one's station. The opportunities for getting ahead were almost non-existent.

The industrial revolution in the late 18th century changed all that. Along with providing us with new products and technologies, the era ushered in a world of opportunities for almost anyone to make money – in some cases, a lot of it. Not surprisingly, power began to shift from those who *had* money, to those who could *make* money.

As early as the 1300s, the idea of shared ownership in business ventures had been put into practice. For large ventures, such as building ocean-faring ships, fractional ownership not only reduced the risk that any one merchant had to take on, but also permitted ship building to be undertaken by more than just the wealthiest. Gradually the idea of shared ownership grew, and "shares" of companies became a tool with which to build wealth.

While the first "stock exchange" was founded in Holland in the early 1600s, it was during the 1800s that the trading of shares became a big business with the development and growth of stock exchanges in New York, London, and many other countries. Still, until quite recently, owning shares remained largely the domain of the wealthy. The complexities of stock ownership, along with accessibility to the market, remained a barrier to entry for the average citizen.

Then came the **mutual fund.** Historians give credit to King William I of Netherlands with the invention of closed-end funds (funds that "trade" based on buy and sell bids) in 1822. But the real progress in opening the doors of the investment world to the masses took place in the U.S. during the thirties with the development of open-end funds, which we know today as investments that can be bought and sold at current prices at any time.

The growth of the mutual fund industry tracks very closely with the ups and downs of the world's markets. With the hyper-growth in the late 80s and 90s, they have become the investment of choice for many Canadians.

But this only partly explains why in a matter of a few decades the number of investors has grown from "very few" to "practically everyone." Today's investor has at his fingertips more information about investing than even existed a few short years ago. And our class structure is no longer carved in stone. The peasant born in the middle ages had little opportunity to become a Lord; today, the riches of the upper class are potentially available to anyone. A good education, and hard work is one way. A far faster, easier ticket of course is the next big run up of that perfect investment.

If history has a lesson to teach us about investing, it would be that the masses tend to get it wrong. Every stock market crash including the "Tech Wreck" of 2000 reveals the same story: human beings simply can't resist the lure of making a quick buck. The lesson is also always the same. This is a sucker's game. There may be a few who win big, but for every one of those, there are **hundreds** who **lose.**

The simple lesson

As of the end of 2005, there were 62 Canadian Equity mutual funds with a history of at least 15 years.[1] Of those funds, only one had a fifteen-year average compound annual return of less than 7%, and 52 of them had returns in excess of 8%. If you had chosen the median fund (the number 31 ranked fund), your 15-year return would have been over 10%. The fact is then, you could have picked just one, and almost *any* one Canadian equity fund 15 years ago, and if you had simply kept that fund through bull markets and bear markets you would have experienced a healthy or even an exceptional return. If you had invested in the median fund your money would have grown by more than 400% over that 15 year period.

Despite the simplicity of this strategy – and the obvious success you would have enjoyed – it's unlikely that anyone actually realized this return. According to a study done in the U.S. by Dalbar, a U.S. based research firm, between 1984 and 2002 the average return on U.S. equity funds during that period was 9.3%. During the same period the average return for U.S. investors was 2.6%. How could this be? It's simple – investors didn't stay with any one fund for too long. They moved their dollars around, or converted to cash after a correction or downturn. As a result, they experienced disastrous underperformance.

The most important thing you can do if you want to be a successful investor is to do nothing.

That's right. Nothing.

Don't sell. Don't switch. Don't convert to cash. Don't dump a fund simply because you think that the manager has underperformed. Leave your investments alone. Maybe then, you can realize some of those excellent long term returns.

---

[1] According to Morningstar, the largest mutual fund rating service in North America.

Putting the lesson to work

Obviously, before you leave your investments alone, you have to chose what they are. And it's also likely that you will be adding to your investments on a regular basis – perhaps making new decisions in light of changing long term plans. So before we get to the stage of doing nothing, we have to do some work, and make some difficult decisions.

Although there are countless types of investments, it helps to classify them into one of three basic asset classes: cash, fixed income, and equity.

Cash

Cash is just that. Think of it as a bank account. You will earn a little interest on your money, and that's it. The advantages to cash are twofold. First, it's safe. Second, it's available when you need it. In the investment business, we call that being liquid. As well as bank accounts, money market funds, and treasury bills (T-bills) issued by governments also form part of this asset group.

Fixed income

Fixed income investments are those that generate a fixed amount of interest income over a specified period of time. Among fixed income investments, the most easily understood (and most popular with Canadians) is the Guaranteed Investment Certificate (GIC). But also included in this category are bonds issued either by governments or by corporations. Like a GIC, bonds pay a specified interest rate, often called a coupon, annually up to a specific date, usually called the maturity date. But unlike GICs, they can be bought and sold on the open market, causing their current value to fluctuate. If bought or sold other than when they are originally issued, it's also likely that their ultimate return, or yield, will be different than the original return.

Equity

Equity is essentially ownership in a corporation. When you buy a share of Bell Canada you become one of millions of people who literally own the company. If you own 10 shares of ABC Corporation, and there are 1,000 shares

MEET JUNE AND KEVIN ALLISTAIR

June and Kevin Allistair were already retired when they first met me - June from 28 years of nursing, and Kevin from 31 years with a large company. Both had pensions, and between them about $300,000 in assets accumulated in registered and open accounts.

Based on their financial plan, which included projected expenses in the "dream" category, they needed very little return – less than 3% in fact - on their investments to see them safely to age 95, and many years beyond. However, their investments were almost 75% in equities, which would suggest a projected return of 7% to 8%. I questioned this and challenged them to consider a investment account comprised of nothing but GICs. In other words, why take risk, when none is needed?

June immediately jumped on the idea of no risk and quickly volunteered that her portion of the portfolio should move to GICs right away. Kevin wasn't sure.

Their money personality profiles revealed some important information. June indeed was a low-risk investor. Kevin on the other hand had scores that suggested he enjoyed the process of selecting investments, and furthermore, was relatively unaffected when markets drop. He not only could stay the course on the downward trip, but enjoyed the ride!

The ultimate resolution to the problem went like this: June's funds were locked away in the safe and secure environment of a laddered GIC portfolio. She was happy. Kevin remained in a balanced portfolio of funds that would be seen as "growing over the long term" to benefit their 3 children and 8 grandchildren.

In our meetings since, we spend 95% of the time talking about family, and 5% of the time affirming the commitment to this strategy. This for me is the sure sign that the strategy is right on track.

in total issued to shareholders, then you own 1% of the company. You stand to benefit in two ways. First, the company may pay a dividend to shareholders from time to time – which is essentially a distribution of profits. Second, if the company is able to grow its profits, the share value should also grow. For example suppose your 10 shares in ABC Corporation cost you $7 each – so your total investment was $70. They may pay you a 14 cent dividend each year, which is 2% of your investment. And, if profits rise and the dividend increases to say 20 cents, other investors may be willing to pay a higher price for the shares. If you were able to sell your shares on the open market for $9 each, or $90, you would make a profit of $20, or 28.5% on your original investment. This $20 profit is called a "capital gain" as it is the gain realized on the sale of an investment.

Over investment periods of 10 years or more, the return on equities should outperform the other asset classes – usually by a significant amount. But as is always the case in the investment world, the potential for greater return carries with it greater risks. Companies don't always increase profits. Sometimes they can experience significant setbacks, potentially even bankruptcy.

In summary, here are the three classes, and the potential risks associated with each:

ASSET CLASS	POTENTIAL RETURN	RISKS
Cash	Rate of inflation (approx 3% historically).	Falling behind financially due to the erosion caused by inflation. Highly taxed. No tax deferral.
Fixed Income	2% to 3% over inflation (approx 5% to 6% historically).	Lower returns may not allow you to realize financial objectives. Interest rate fluctuations will cause bond holdings to fluctuate in value. Highly taxed.
Equity	5% or more over inflation (historically 8% to 10% in Canada).	Share prices fluctuate – often dramatically, and carry the risk of losing value over short periods.

So, how should **you** invest?

First, separate long-term and short-term investments. Any money you expect to use in five years or less should really be invested mostly, if not entirely, in cash. Certainly with equities (and even with bonds), the risk of experiencing a loss within a five-year period outweighs the potential for higher returns. GICs are a possibility, but if you need the money in less than five years you may find that the appropriate term of the GIC carries with it a rate that is lower than a high interest bank account (cash), making it an unattractive option. Five years or less, think cash.

Long-term investments then should ideally be divided between fixed income and equities. The question is, in what proportion?

That will depend largely on two factors.

> 1) How much risk you *need* to take in order to realize your financial objectives.
> 2) How much risk you *want* to take based on your unique money personality.

To answer number 1, you need to do some planning. Or find yourself a financial planner who can help you crunch the numbers. What you are looking for is the rate of return – that should be somewhere between 3% (cash) and 8%+ (equities) – that will allow you to accumulate the funds you need in the time frame you have established. There are other variables of course. You can adjust the amount you save each year, or the total amount of money to accumulate, or your investment time frame. Your willingness to push return rates higher in order to accomplish goals needs to be directly proportional to your willingness to take risks as established in point number two.

And that's not **easy** to measure.

The risk profiling tools used by most financial institutions place their emphasis on time horizon and net worth, rather than on understanding how we *feel* about seeing assets decline. One tool that does a surprisingly good job of this is the Moneymax Financial Profile, which can be found at **www.kathleengurney.com.** The score on this test that reveals what Kathleen calls "self-determination" is an excellent guide with respect to whether you can handle a more aggressive portfolio.

What this score is all about is the feeling of **control.** Let's suppose you buy shares in ABC Mutual Fund and for the first few months they start to rise. You feel good about that. You are making money, and you are convinced you made a good investment. But then, disaster happens and the share prices plummet. They fall consistently for many days, then weeks, possibly months and you gradually see your profits, and then your initial investment dwindle away. Now how do you feel? If your automatic response is something like "Just my luck!", or, "I'm probably going to lose all my money!", then you would score low on the self-determination score. If you feel totally out of control in these situations then your instincts will scream at you to sell the investment. And more often than not, that's the wrong thing to do. Your portfolio should be low on equity content.

If on the other hand you say something like "This is a good solid investment fund that will bounce back. I'm not too concerned. This is a long term investment," then you obviously continue to feel in control. You will most likely keep the investment, and perhaps even consider investing more, if you have the cash to do so. You would score high on the self-determination score. Equities are for you.

Most people fall somewhere in between these extremes. For these people careful consideration must be given to how much equity is included in the portfolio, and what they expect to do when (not if) equities fall in value. The first step in dealing with the risk of market volatility is to realize that it is certain to occur.

Once we have determined the appropriate return rate based on our needs and our willingness to experience greater volatility, we can establish our "asset mix." This is simply an exercise in determining how much of each asset class we should carry in our portfolio in order to achieve the desired long term return.

ARE YOU A PASSIVE OR AN ACTIVE INVESTOR?

One of the great debates in the investment fund world is the debate over indexing, commonly phrased as the fight between passive investing and managed investing. All stock markets of the world have indexes comprised of a basket of securities that are intended to represent the entire market. In Toronto, the S&P TSX Composite index, which contains some 200+ securities, is the standard by which economists and analysts measure the overall performance of Canada's stock market.

For Canadian equity fund managers, this is often the "benchmark" by which they are measured as well. If their returns exceed the benchmark they are said to "add value," and if their returns fall short, then their value is questioned. Many analysts will suggest that investing in a managed fund is a waste of money as most managers fail to outperform their respect indexes. Index funds, which replicate the securities of the index and therefore involve no actual skill or effort, can be purchased for very little cost relative to managed funds.

But this debate *always* misses the point.

It is true that when measuring overall returns, the index will most often beat more than half of all fund managers. As of November 30, 2005, there were 286 Canadian equity funds with at least a five year track record as reported by Morningstar. Based on returns, highest to lowest, the S&P TSX Composite ranked 133rd. That means it beat roughly 55% of the managed funds over the past five years. But, based on five year Standard Deviation numbers, it was the 42nd most volatile fund in this group – meaning that 86% of the fund managers added value by reducing volatility. In fact, only 29 of the managers failed to beat the index on one of the two scores – so almost 90% of the managers added value in some way.

Of course, most managers will underperform the index when the markets are growing rapidly, and out-perform when markets are falling. In other words, they lag behind when things are really good, preferring instead to move ahead more cautiously, and then when things get bad their caution pays off.

Here's the bottom line: Using index funds instead of managed funds isn't better, or worse. It's just different. The question is: which investment will you most likely hang onto during difficult times? Choose that one. In my experience, when things are bad, most people take comfort knowing that a manager is helping to soften the blow – and perhaps even taking steps to buy securities that have been beaten down – which improves returns on the bounce back up.

For example, if we determine that our target return is 7%, we may consider the following weightings:

ASSET CLASS	LONG-TERM RETURN	WEIGHTING
Cash	3%	0%
Fixed Income	5%	30%
Equity	8%	70%
	EXPECTED LONG-TERM RETURN:	7.1%

The 7.1% long term expected return is derived from multiplying the weighting of each asset class by its long term return and then adding them together. If for example we weighted our portfolio 100% to equities, the long term expected return would be 8%. The other groups cause the return to decrease as their returns are lower, but they also add stability to the portfolio as their volatility is lower as well.

Now comes the **difficult** part – selecting the individual securities that make up our investment portfolio. There are thousands of companies listed on various stock exchanges around the world, and a similar number of bonds. How do we choose a particular company? Should we buy corporate bonds or government bonds, and should we choose long term or short term bonds?

If you are a true "do-it-yourselfer" then dig in, learn all you can, make some choices, pay attention to your investments on a regular basis, and good luck. This of course is far from simple. For the rest of us there's a simple solution – hire an investment manager.

Ideally we want an investment manager who is among the best: a seasoned veteran with a proven track-record, devoting 100% to the task at hand, with access to the best information to ensure that nothing is overlooked.

We have entered the world of **investment funds.**

HAVE YOU "OUTGROWN" INVESTMENT FUNDS?

Once your portfolio grows to a certain size, you will eventually hear someone say "You've outgrown investment funds, it's time to get into _____." This implies that the average Canadian is somehow unable to obtain the kind of investment management afforded those considered wealthy. Investment funds in fact are the great equalizer – providing access to some of the best managers in the world for as little as $25 per month!

The legitimate concern here is cost, not strategy, and it's an issue that is easily overcome without sacrificing the benefits of a well-diversified investment fund portfolio. Almost all investment funds come in a variety of "share classes," each with a different cost structure. As your account grows, you should be eligible to move to a lower cost structure. Most notable are "F-class" shares, which strip out the advisor compensation allowing that advisor to add back a lower compensation level to recognize the account size. Beyond that there's "Institutional-class" shares, which are offered to pension funds and other institutions at substantially lower costs again. If you believe you are in the big leagues, don't ask your advisor to switch strategies. Ask if there is a plan to adjust your costs as your account size grows.

I am using the term investment funds here to include a wide range of products, from the most popular mutual funds and segregated funds to wrap accounts and pooled funds.

Investment fund managers have one job: to make you money. A fund manager for a particular fund is given a mandate – essentially a set of rules that they must follow in choosing investments for the fund. For example, some managers will invest only in large Canadian companies, some in a mix of Canadian stocks and bonds, others in foreign stocks. The possibilities are endless. The tighter the mandate, the more restricted the manager's choices.

Despite the fact that mutual funds were created in part to simplify the investment choices for the average investor, the proliferation of funds has made choosing them anything but simple. Which funds should you consider? How many funds do you need to build a diversified portfolio? Good questions. Allow me to provide some answers.

MEET GINNETTE THORNTON

Ginnette Thornton had some money to invest, but was clearly afraid to make a decision. Her mind, and often her voice, raced with potential troubles. Maybe this was the wrong time! Maybe the market will drop! Maybe interest rates will rise! Her conclusion was always the same - let's wait and see.

Finally, she decided to put 10% of her money into a portfolio of funds that I had recommended, but she added, "I'll see how this does over the next little while and if I'm getting good returns I may put in some more."

Instead of asking her to write a cheque, I asked her to consider the only possibilities there were. "What will you do if the market goes down?"

"Probably pull this money out."

"And if the market goes up?"

"Probably put more money in."

"And if the market goes nowhere?"

"Wait and see."

I pointed out that this was precisely the strategy employed by the masses, who usually get it wrong to a spectacular degree.

Her money profile showed a low score in "self-determination," meaning that her feelings would indeed be strong enough when things are bad to cause her to react and sell low. So I suggested the following:

First of all, she was to take out the money she may need over the next 5 years. This it turns out was about 10% of the total – and this portion went into a high interest bank account. Next, we would take the remaining amount and split it into two equal pots – each representing 45% of the total. We would invest one portion into a laddered GIC portfolio – staggering the terms equally from 1 to 5 years. The other portion we would invest in a wrap account, of primarily equity funds, using a segregated fund with a 100% guarantee in 10 years. (There's more on segregated funds elsewhere in this chapter.)

Now, in 10 years, in a worst-case scenario, our investment returns would be the GIC rates (hovering around 3.5% at the time of the discussion) on the GIC portion, and 0% on the segregated fund. Combining the two, and we would at worst experience a return of roughly 1.75% overall.

But, the wrap account had a potential return of 7%, so if things went well, our overall return might be 5.25%, and possibly higher.

Now she started thinking in terms of a range of returns, rather than extremes. She also started to think long term – using 5 year time frames on the GICs and the 10 years to maturity on the segregated funds. The cushion of cash left her feeling secure that short term needs would be met, no matter what the state of her investments at the time. We went ahead with the plan.

Many analysts would argue vehemently against this plan for many reasons. For example, the fees on segregated funds are too high – paying for the guarantee is a waste of money since we have never had a losing 10 year period in equities. And GIC rates are too low – we should put more in equities, or use bonds instead.

But all of these criticisms fail to consider the most important aspect of all – the client's personality. The objective of this portfolio is to generate returns that are acceptable to the client, in a fashion that will enable them to stay put when things get tough.

The market will go down – probably several times – during the next ten years for Ginette. If the seg fund and GIC mix allows her to rationalize that "someone else" is taking on the risk and therefore causes her to stay the course during that time, then the right product was used – and the extra fees were well spent. 5.2% is significantly better than the returns she would have generated using her sell when things are down, and buy when things go up strategy. And that's the goal – realize the best possible results, based on what the individual is willing, and *able* to do.

Choosing funds

The number one criterion for choosing investment funds is to choose the funds you will stick with when (not if) they look like the wrong choice in the future. With analytical tools aplenty, and rating services and authors purporting to be able to separate the good from the bad, it is easy to conclude that we should be able to find the "best" fund in every category. But looking for the best fund is a recipe for disaster. Rest assured that some other fund will surprise everyone and hit number one in its category at some future point in time. And if you are indeed intent on owning the best fund, you will feel compelled to switch – and lower returns are most likely to be the result.

So how do we find these "good" funds? We need to choose funds we will stay committed to. It may be a particular fund manager or fund company that we trust. It may be those funds that have experienced good long term results with respect to returns and volatility. And, we should build a portfolio of different funds to help us feel positive about things when some of our funds appear to be moving in the wrong direction.

Again, looking at funds with a long term track record, very few exhibit poor long term returns. It would appear that we can choose almost any fund and expect a decent long term annual compound return – for a Canadian equity fund for example, something in the range of 8%. But, that fund is going to experience many ups and downs along the way – much like the following graph.

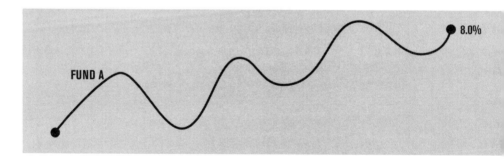

Fund A wiggles its way to a healthy 8% return. We naturally feel pretty good about this fund when its on one of its upward climbs, but during the downtrends, especially if they are lengthy, we are no doubt going to feel insecure about our choice. And if this were the only fund we owned, it would be extremely difficult to stay on board. In fact, as the statistics commonly show, most people will be the most unhappy (and hence sell the fund) just prior to the next big run up.

Diversification is all about dealing with this issue. The ultimate goal of diversification is to smooth the road as much as possible. Consider the combination of Fund A and Fund B.

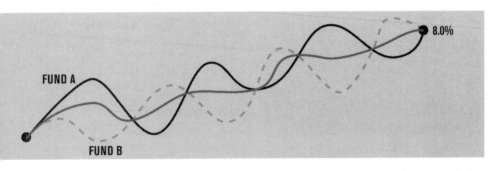

If we could find Fund B, that ended up with the same return, but traveled generally in the opposite direction to Fund A, we could use 50% of each fund to produce a near straight line return of 8%!

Of course, in the real world, finding Fund A and B that offer this near-perfect negative correlation is almost impossible. But, it is possible to find funds that provide diversification – funds that when combined will reduce the volatility of the overall portfolio, without sacrificing returns. This is the objective of constructing a portfolio of funds, and the criteria upon which you can do this are as follows: asset class, geography, market capitalization, and management style.

Asset class

As already discussed, the three main asset classes are cash, fixed income, and equity, and your weighting in each will be determined largely by your need for a given return matched with your desire and ability to withstand volatility.

After several years of strong equity performance, it is tempting to consider yourself capable of taking on more risk. Be careful. Know who you are, and consider what you will feel and the actions you are likely to contemplate if equity

LADDERING GICS

If you are investing in GICs it is important to create a strategy that will allow you to disengage from the process of trying to predict interest rate movements. A GIC ladder is just that.

The concept is fairly simple: Take your total GIC portfolio and divide it into five equal parts, and invest each part into a GIC of different durations so that they mature in 1, 2, 3, 4 and 5 years. Each year, as one portion matures, invest that into a new five year GIC so that once again you have funds maturing each year for the next five. After five years, all five portions will be invested in five-year terms and the process continues until you need the money for some other purpose.

The elegance of this strategy comes from its simplicity. No thinking is required. Since you have funds re-investing every year, each year you can either be happy to be reinvesting at a new higher rate, or happy to have 80% of your money not renewing as rates have come down!

markets drop by 15%, 25% or more. Invest accordingly. Use fixed income funds to reduce overall volatility and help you stay the course when things are rough.

Geography

During the five years prior to the market crash in 2000, Canadians were doing all they could to shift their investments outside Canada and into the United States. The U.S. market, lead by the high tech sector, was racing ahead, and those promoting foreign investments used the high return numbers along with the rally cry "Canada is only 3% of the global market!" to steer Canadians into red hot U.S. stocks. By the turn of the century, Canadian investment in the U.S. market was peaking. The image of lemmings running madly to the edge and then over the cliff comes to mind.

Then in the year 2000 the tide turned. For the 6 years up to and including 2005 one of the best markets in the world has been Canada – far outpacing our neighbour to the south. Gradually investors have moved away from foreign markets, and into Canadian investments – in particular those investments considered more secure – like bond funds, and cash, or those that appeared to be more secure, like income trusts. Heading into 2006, the underweight position was clearly global investments, and despite the cry from analysts who have been touting the importance of diversifying globally, investors resist moving into this underperforming category. It would seem that the lesson, so harshly taught in the late 1990s about diversifying geographically, has yet to be learned.

The point is this: sometimes Canadian investments are best, sometimes U.S. investments are best, and sometimes other markets are best. No-one can accurately predict which is next, but in time **each** will take its turn at the **top** (and at the **bottom**).

In order to be in the right geographical region at any time, one needs to be in all geographical regions all the time. A balanced portfolio should always contain a healthy amount of Canadian funds, along with a reasonable representation in U.S. and international funds.

When choosing foreign funds that are labeled "global," it is important to assess the geographical diversification of the particular fund in order to accurately determine your overall diversification. Most global funds have a large weighting in U.S. stocks, which if ignored, can shift your portfolio weighting too much into the U.S. and too little in other countries around the world. You may want to consider using funds which invest exclusively outside North America to ensure a balanced distribution around the globe.

Market capitalization

The market capitalization (market cap) of a company is simply the total value of the company as determined by multiplying the current share price by the total number of shares on record. For example, if ABC Corporation has 100 million shares in total, and the current share price is $10, then the "market cap" of the company is $1 billion.

The largest companies on any exchange are called "large cap" stocks. These are usually the big names we recognize – in Canada they include the big banks, life insurance companies, oil and gas firms, etc. - and they are generally measured in the tens and hundreds of billions of dollars. Sometimes referred to as "blue chip" stocks, these companies are perceived to be the safest, but also the slowest-growing stocks on the market.

Companies at the other end of the spectrum are called "small cap" stocks. In general, they are more quickly able to adapt to customer needs and therefore will sometimes experience more explosive growth. We seldom recognize their names, but are attracted to their upside potential. It is important to note that these are not really "small" companies. The market cap of the smallest companies on most markets will be measured in hundreds of millions of dollars.

In the middle of course come the "mid cap" stocks. These are often companies that are growing, or companies that are in smaller sectors of the economy. Their market cap will generally range in the billions, but they are many times smaller than the largest companies on the market.

Similarly to geographical regions, small, large and mid-cap stocks will perform differently at different times in the market cycle. Trying to guess which will be hot from year to year is a sucker's game. So again, a well-diversified portfolio will contain some stocks ranging across the market cap spectrum. As always, we need to keep risk in mind, and as our tolerance for volatility reduces, we should also reduce our holdings in small and mid cap stocks.

Management style

When it comes to picking stocks, managers generally favour one of two distinct styles:
growth or value.

The value manager is looking for stocks that are selling at what they perceive to be a discount price, far below "true intrinsic value." Some, known as "deep value" managers go so far as to say they are looking for stocks that have been discarded by the rest of the investment world. Often, the stocks purchased by value managers continue to decline, and usually they will eagerly buy more. Most people aren't encouraged when they learn their manager has just purchased stocks that are in decline. And most investors lack the patience to wait and see if things turn out in the end. This means that value managers are at times an unpopular choice.

The growth manager on the other hand focuses his attention on companies that show signs of near-term or long-term growth. Changes at the company level, or

WHAT YOU NEED TO KNOW ABOUT SEGREGATED FUNDS

In most respects, segregated (seg) funds are exactly the same as mutual funds. In fact, most of the largest retail mutual funds can also be purchased as a seg fund. The differences lie in the fact that seg funds are offered by insurance companies, and include some advantages that are only afforded the insurance industry. The notable advantages are: guarantees, probate avoidance, and creditor protection.

The guarantees on seg funds come in two forms: a maturity guarantee and a death benefit guarantee. On most funds, the maturity period is 10 years, and the guarantee is either 100% of deposits, or 75% of deposits, with the higher guarantee incurring a higher fee. The maturity guarantee can often be "reset" to allow the investor to lock-in gains, while at the same time extending their maturity time frame to 10 years from that point. This guarantee provides some comfort to the investor who feels less than secure about the risk of equity investments. It's important to note however that for most stock markets history is void of any losing 10 year periods, so the guarantee is protecting the investor from a scenario that has yet to happen.

The death benefit guarantee provides for a similar guarantee, usually 100%, to occur on the death of the investor. So if you invested $10,000 into ABC Seg Fund, and the market drops by 25%, and in your despair you die of a failing heart, your beneficiaries would receive the full $10,000 despite the market value of your investments being only $7,500. This is a particularly attractive feature for seniors who are not only planning for their own future, but likely also planning for the transfer of wealth to family.

Along the same theme, on death, seg fund assets can be directed to a named beneficiary directly. Since they bypass the will, they won't be subject to probate and legal costs associated with administering an estate. This is no small benefit, considering how large an investment account can grow.

For those concerned about potential bankruptcy, or legal issues that may lead them in that direction, seg funds are also protected from creditors.

A word of caution – all of these benefits are derived from specific legal interpretations of the various acts governing insurance products, and while they have been adequately tested and proven to work, there are specific situations in which they may not. Getting help to ensure they are properly set up is strongly advised.

The notable downside to seg funds is cost – due to the guarantees, the MER on similar funds will be .5% to 1% higher, and sometimes more, in the segregated fund version. Even with the extra cost, for many investors they make a great deal of sense and are worthy of consideration.

perhaps in the industry, or even in the economy, will give the growth manager clues about what may happen next to a company's share price. While they would never ignore value, growth managers simply believe that it is a less important criterion.

So, as a company's price falls, the value manager gets interested. If it falls below the perceived intrinsic value set by the value manager, she will start buying. The growth manager has yet to put this company on the radar. As prices continue to fall, the value manager keeps buying, and at this stage she appears to be dramatically underperforming her growth counterparts, who are either clinging on to cash, or moving in and out of a few companies that are experiencing some growth. The attention of investors shifts to growth.

When stock prices start to rise, value managers suddenly look good again. At some point on the rise of a company's share price, the growth manager is likely to hop on board. Both growth and value are rolling along. Soon however, the value manager gets concerned – the price is now above her intrinsic value, and she sells, and begins looking for bargains again. Usually, the growth manager remains on board, so long as there remains reasonable potential for growth. When stock prices turn and head down, sometimes quickly, the growth manager is likely still left with a number of positions that he was unable to sell in time. The growth manager's portfolio is likely to fall hard. Meanwhile the value manager is busy collecting undervalued stocks, and sitting on piles of cash in order to do so, and her portfolio drops very little. Investors' interest turns to value.

While this is an oversimplification, it serves to illustrate the essential difference between these two management styles, and also helps us to understand why we see such dramatic differences in relative performance at different stages of the economic cycle.

Which is better? Over long periods of time, the two styles
show very little difference in return. The growth style however exhibits much more volatility. It is therefore wise for the more conservative investor to overweight value. But, once again, true diversification, which reduces the overall volatility of the portfolio, is only achieved when both styles are represented.

INVESTING AND TAXES

If your investments are inside a registered plan, (such as an RRSP), then the tax implications of an investment are irrelevant. Inside the plan, no tax is payable. When assets are removed from the plan, the entire amount is treated as "income" and taxed at your marginal rate.

Outside of registered plans, or in "open" plans, the tax treatment of individual investments are important to understand and take into consideration. There are three forms of income that be derived from an investment: interest, dividend, and capital gains.

Interest income, which is earned on GICs, bonds, and bank accounts, is taxed in the same manner as your earned income. $1 of interest is equal to $1 of taxable income.

Dividend income, which is earned on some (not all) company stocks, is taxed more favourably. A formula, established by CRA, essentially reduces the tax on dividends by at least 30% or more relative to earned income. (The actual reduction depends on your total taxable income, with a more favourable reduction at lower income levels.) In this case then, you might consider $1 of dividend income as equal to only 70 cents, or less, of taxable income.

Capital gains receive the most favourable tax treatment of all. As stock prices increase, the difference between your purchase price (what we financial types call your adjusted cost base) and the current price is considered a capital gain. If you bought a share of ABC Corp for $10 and it has a current price of $13, you have a gain of $3. Capital gains are included as regular income when calculating tax, but only 50% of the capital gain is considered taxable. Further, only gains that are "realized," are taxable. Year to year as your stock grows in value, the increase in value is not included in your taxable income. In this case, the tax is considered "deferred." When you sell the stock, and realize the gain, the tax becomes payable – but on a capital gain of $1, only 50 cents is considered a "taxable capital gain."

Clearly, capital gains and dividends are preferred ways to earn income from investments. But pursuing capital gains and dividends requires us to own company stocks, which is the most volatile form of investing. Low risk and high return are always at opposite ends of the spectrum – and in our attempts to find the right place for us, we end up with a balanced portfolio.

FEES AND COMMISSIONS

All investments have a cost. The important thing to understand about investment funds is how to determine and compare that cost to similar products.

Investment fund fees are usually referred to as the MER (Management Expense Ratio), comprised of four distinct costs.

a) Management expenses, covering the costs of the fund manager, research, marketing costs and profit to the fund management company;

b) Dealer/advisor compensation, including the costs of compliance and the administration services of the dealer as well as the fee paid to an advisor who is working with the client to achieve long-term goals;

c) Administrative costs, including regulatory expenses, processing costs, reporting, custody, audit and legal fees;

d) Taxes (GST).

Add those up and the costs of operating an investment fund in Canada generally will be close to:

Canadian money market funds	0.71%
Canadian bond funds	1.45%
Canadian balanced funds	2.12%
Canadian equity funds	2.44%
Global equity funds	2.51%

(The numbers represent a % of the assets charged every year.)

It is important to note that by law, when you see the stated returns of an investment fund in Canada, that return is stated "net" of the fees. That means the return you see is your actual return, after the fee has been paid.

Another important issue to understand about investment fund fees is what we normally call "loads." There are essentially three load structures to know about: back end load, front end load, and no load. The back end load model, often referred to as DSC (deferred sales charge) has been for many years the most popular model used by advisors. In this scenario, when your funds are invested, the dealer is paid an up front commission, usually 5% of your investment in the case of an equity fund, which is shared between the dealer and the advisor. 100% of your money however is invested into the fund – you don't pay this commission. You are then placed onto a DSC schedule that outlines the "penalty" you would pay should you extract your money from that fund family within a specified time. Usually the penalty starts at 6% in year one, and declines to 0% in year seven.

This arrangement provides the opportunity for you to invest essentially without paying the "load," and still provides the advisor with compensation up front to offset the usually higher costs of developing plans and transferring assets at the outset of a relationship. Of course, it's not perfect. Should you require your funds earlier than expected, the bite of the penalty is often nasty. In an effort to provide you with some flexibility, all fund companies allow you to extract up to 10% of your assets in any year without penalty.

All funds that are sold on a DSC basis can also be sold on a front end basis. In this scenario, the advisor and you agree to an up front fee, typically between 0% and 5%, that you will pay so as not to be subject to a DSC schedule thereafter.

Understand that almost all funds sold on a DSC basis or front end basis have the exact same MER in either case. A few funds and fund families deviate from this rule, so you should check with your advisor to make sure you are getting the least expensive fund.

No load funds are just that, funds without loads. Many advisors will use regular funds on a "front end zero" basis – that is, they use the front end load version, but set your fee at 0%. This is essentially setting your investment up on a no load basis.

Finally, almost all funds pay a "trailer fee" to the dealer, which is also shared with the advisor. This fee is an ongoing commission based on a % of assets. In most cases, for DSC funds, the trailer fee is .5%, on equity funds. If the same fund is set up with a front end load, the trailer bumps to 1%. Even most no load fund families provide a trailer fee (although usually lower than the trailer offered by others) to encourage advisors to use their funds. Some do not. If you are hoping to align your goals with that of your advisor, you should be prepared to negotiate a fair arrangement. The trailer fee does align your goals pretty well. The ongoing commission compensates your advisor for the continuing work done on your behalf, and grows as your account grows.

How do you tell which style a manager is using? For the average investor, this may be one of the more difficult aspects of a mutual fund to measure, and unfortunately the labeling of mutual funds is sometimes misleading. Start by looking on-line at one of the fund rating services websites – in Canada that might be Morningstar, or GlobeFund. You can also call the mutual fund company directly. Or ask your advisor.

It's important to note that most managers fall somewhere in between growth and value, combining the two into a style of their own. In fact, a hybrid of these two, growth-at-a-reasonable-price (GARP), is perhaps the most common style of all. Still, managers will tend to lean in one direction or the other, and there are managers out there who do ride on the edges of each style.

Portfolio building

A sample diversified portfolio may look something like this:

25% Canadian bond fund
15% Canadian equity large cap value
15% Canadian equity large cap growth
10% Canadian equity small cap
15% Global equity all cap growth
10% U.S. equity large cap value
10% International equity large cap GARP

Usually, seven to nine funds will provide complete diversification. If there's a fund you just "have to own," because it has been so hot lately, add it on and keep its weighting to 5%. Most likely, you will be happy that you didn't invest more.

Picking the specific funds

Now that we know what kinds of funds we are looking for to put into our portfolio, we can search for the right fund in each category. This isn't really as difficult as it may seem. Begin by narrowing the universe of choices down to a few that fall into each category. In the Canadian equity large cap value category for example, you may narrow the field down by taking the top funds based on five year (or longer) returns, lowest measures of volatility, and perhaps lowest costs (Management Expense Ratio – MER). Whittle it down to five or so funds, and now choose any of them.

Keep in mind the simple lesson: the investments you

choose, you need to hang onto, even when it looks like selling is the right thing to do. Make your choices accordingly. Learn whatever you need to know in order to make a choice you can live with. Or at least choose an advisor who is willing to hold funds for the long term. Beware the advisor who leads you to believe that he or she can "adjust" your portfolio each year in order to catch the next great thing. If you have done a good job of diversifying, you will always find funds in your portfolio that you are happy about, and funds that are disappointing. If you attempt to eject the disappointments you will invariably be following the path of

A BRIEF WORD ON DISCRETIONARY MANAGEMENT

A discretionary account is an investment account in which you hand over the controls to an investment manager. He or she will choose the individual securities that will go into your account, and buy and sell as they see fit on an ongoing basis. Really, this is what any investment fund manager does. The difference is that in a discretionary account, the investment manager has met with you and is supposed to choose the securities to suit your specific long term goals and money personality. You might think of it as a "personalized" investment fund.

Is this better than investment funds? It usually will offer the advantage of lower costs – at least as compared to regular retail funds. On the negative side, choosing a discretionary account generally means that you are now counting on the performance of one manager, instead of several.

Really, choosing this type of investment strategy over a portfolio of funds has much more to do with your personality than anything else. If you want more control, and some input into the individual security selection – discretionary management may be for you. If you are looking for the simple solution with minimum hassles, then stick with funds.

"sell low and buy high," and your ultimate returns will weaken. Look at your portfolio and tell yourself that those underperformers are keeping you diversified. Add to them as necessary to keep them balanced in your portfolio. One day they are going to be your best funds.

It's really that simple. Choose good funds that each bring something unique to your portfolio. Rebalance as you add new dollars into the portfolio to keep your weightings near your targets.

Watch your money **grow** over time.

If you are looking for the absolute in simplicity – in other words the lowest level of involvement on your part, all of this can be accomplished by choosing just one investment account. Commonly referred to as a "wrap" program, but sometimes called an "asset allocation portfolio" or a "fund of funds," this all-in-one program follows all of the steps described here to choose individual funds that coordinate to form an optimally diversified portfolio aimed at achieving the highest possible returns with the lowest possible risk. The limitation on this kind of portfolio – the fact that you are unable to tinker with the individual components yourself – will in fact prove to be a valuable benefit, as it prevents you from acting on the impulse to sell your worst performing funds in order to buy more of your best.

In the past, these wrap programs have been criticized for underperformance and high fees. To a large degree, the underperformance can be attributed to the management company's failure to consider a wide enough universe of funds, often choosing just from a short list of their own fund managers. Today, most wraps involve a wide range of managers who are carefully monitored to ensure that they are the "best of the best." As for fees, they have come down considerably and many excellent wraps can be purchased for a marginal additional cost. Given the fact that experts are being called on to develop the portfolios and rebalancing services ensure that your holdings remain at optimal levels without you or an advisor manually shifting assets, this extra fee is well justified.

Those looking for simple solutions to their investment needs are being extraordinarly well served in today's investment world. Despite the complexities of financial products, and the growing number of those products, we can make one decision, and then get on with life. And, for those who make that one decision, this is a great way to eliminate the stress that comes from worrying about whether or not this is the time to be in equities or bonds, in Canada or Japan, in small cap or large cap. After all, the extraordinary life is not one in which we are financial experts – it's one in which we have all of our needs met.

And all of our dreams **fulfilled.**

SIMPLE MONEY

The best thing to do with your investments is nothing. Don't sell or switch, just hang on.

Choosing the right investment funds isn't that difficult. It's hanging on to them when they don't look so good that's tough.

Know your investment personality, and choose investment strategies to suit.

Diversify portfolios by geography, asset class, market capitalization, and management style.

Keep costs to a minimum, but be willing to pay for what you need; things like advice, management, and peace of mind.

EXTRAORDINARY LIFE

Your goal is not to become an investment expert. Your goal is to free your time to pursue the things that are really important; the things that will make your life truly extraordinary.

Chapter 6

Life insurance & estate planning

he greatest gift is the ability to give. And life insurance is best understood when it is seen as a gift.

A brief historical perspective

The history of insurance reaches back at least as far as 1800 BC, when the Chinese developed the practice of "bottomry." The Code of Hammurabi contained some 282 references to bottomry - essentially a loan taken out to finance the voyage of a ship with the understanding that the loan would be forgiven if the ship was lost at sea. Marine insurance was prevalent in many ancient societies, but it was developed into a business as we know it in the late 1600s by Edward Lloyd of London, who, in the coffee shops near the stock exchange, brokered insurance contracts between sea captains and "risk-takers" who would underwrite the ship's cargo by signing their names under the terms of the contract, thus coining the term "underwriter."

As building materials moved from stone to wood another risk presented itself; fire. The great fire of London in 1666 sparked many changes in an attempt to manage this risk including the founding of the first fire insurance company.

The insuring of property is perhaps a more logical and business-like concept than insuring a human life, and so the history of life insurance tends to be sprinkled with more words like "community," "caring," and "assistance." In India as far back as 1000 BC the Vedas (an ancient Hindu scripture) had a form of "community insurance" to provide for one another when a member of the community died. In ancient Rome burial clubs were formed to provide funds for the burial of

deceased members and financial assistance to the survivors. During the middl
ages "guilds" did the same, caring for members who lost a loved one.

Life insurance as we know it today in a business sense also got its start in th
coffee houses of 17th century England. Made illegal almost everywhere in Europe
the life insurance business soared in England during this time, partly due to th
popularity of betting on the lives of the ill, whose names were published in news
papers. Hardly an auspicious start, this practice was made illegal in 1777
About the same time, insurance emerged in the United States, with th
Presbyterian's Ministers Fund issuing the first life insurance policies in 1759 to i
ministers. Life insurance as a business began soon thereafter in the U.S. with th
first policy issued in Philadelphia in 1761.

Both the business of life insurance and the benevolent desire for organizations t
provide assistance to members in time of need grew over the next two centurie.
Life insurance companies expanded their operations, and fraternal groups, rel
gious bodies, and ultimately employers developed policies of providing insuranc
to members and looked after surviving family members; in some cases practice
that continue today.

And yet, the fraternal and religious groups that continue to provide insuranc
solutions to members are finding it increasingly difficult to compete with service
offered by today's large insurance companies. Employers are increasingly down
loading benefits, including life insurance, to employees. Our community it woul
seem has shrunk to mean family. Furthermore, the benefits provide
by employers and government tend to be the bare minimum for surviva
Individuals all strive for higher and higher standards of living and want loved one
who are left behind to do the same. Outside the context of a conventional famil
life insurance today would appear to be **all business.**

The history of insurance – both property and life insurance – show evidence of tw
distinct catalysts: the opportunity for profit, and the desire to look after each othe

in time of need. It is the latter motive, the unselfish desire to help others when help is needed, that more distinctly underpins the history of life insurance. And it is the reason you should consider life insurance as part of your extraordinary life.

The simple lesson

When it comes to discussing life insurance, there are three main questions.

1) Do I need/want life insurance, and if so,
2) how much and
3) what type?

In answer to the first question, there are only **two** reasons to consider owning life insurance.

The first is to manage risk – specifically the risk of dying too soon. The second is to enhance wealth – specifically the wealth of your beneficiaries, in most cases those being spouses, children, and grandchildren.

The most obvious application of life insurance as a risk management tool is to replace the income lost due to the death of a major income earner in a family. If you have a mortgage and young children it may be clear that your family would be financially incapable of carrying on their present lifestyle without your income. Life insurance is the answer.

There are, of course, other applications. For example a lender may want to make sure that the loan can be repaid should the borrower die, and business people may want to protect from potential losses that may occur due to the death of a key partner or employee. In all cases, someone stands to lose financially, perhaps severely, if someone else should die prematurely. This use of insurance isn't about making someone rich should a death occur, but rather, keeping someone whole.

It's about **protection,** not wealth.

WHOSE INVESTMENT IS IT?

In most cases insurance should not be considered an investment for the insured, but rather an investment for the beneficiaries. In that respect it's unparalleled. The tax preferred status of permanent insurance makes it a pretty attractive place to park additional funds. If these funds are intended to be passed on to the beneficiaries there isn't a better investment.

If the insured intends to extract those funds later for personal use, then a comparison should be constructed between the insurance and an investment outside the insurance contract. It is certainly possible to make the insurance an attractive option, but it will likely involve borrowing against the future cash values (as opposed to simply withdrawing funds from the policy). This is not a strategy for everyone – especially those who haven't exhausted their RRSP room, or eliminated personal debt.

The second reason for owning life insurance *is* about wealth. Many pursue wealth not just to enjoy during their own lifetimes, but also so that they may positively affect the lives of the next generation and ideally generations to come. When this becomes a goal, we have entered the realm of estate planning, and life insurance once again becomes a topic worthy of consideration.

Life insurance from an estate planning point of view provides two powerful advantages over other types of financial products. First, it is afforded preferential tax treatment: in Canada, life insurance proceeds are **tax free.**

And equally important, the death benefit arranged becomes part of one's legacy immediately – even if death occurs the next day – providing wealth to the heirs that otherwise may not have existed.

If you have established a desire to own life insurance, you must then consider the appropriate amount. When it comes to life insurance as protection, the answer can be approximated by answering yet another question. If you died tonight how much money would the beneficiaries need to carry on financially as if you were still here?

If you are considering life insurance to enhance the wealth of your beneficiaries, the amount is much more a question of how much you wish to assign to future generations and how much you need to keep on hand for your own use.

And the type? There are only two types of life insurance – term insurance and permanent insurance. The simplest way to understand them is to know that term insurance is intended for risk protection, while permanent insurance is intended for the transfer of wealth to the next generation.

Term insurance, as the name implies, provides a benefit and carries a fixed premium for a specific term. In most cases the person insured hopes to outlive the contract period and thus never collect the death benefit.

Permanent insurance on the other hand terminates only on death with the payout of the benefit amount (unless the insured cancels prior to that). With permanent insurance, the insured plans to realize the death benefit, and is able to look at premiums as being more of an investment for the beneficiaries as opposed to a cost of providing protection.

For most people, the need for insurance follows a **predictable pattern.**

While young with dependents and debts, there is a tremendous risk to the family that requires fairly large amounts of life insurance to protect. Term insurance in appropriate amounts to adequately care for your family is almost always the best solution.

As your dependents become self-sufficient, as wealth accumulates, and as debts disappear, term insurance becomes less important and eventually isn't needed at all.

Then, as you get older, your wealth increases further, and your thoughts turn from "what would happen *if*" questions about death, to "what will happen *when*" questions. You start to consider the value of your assets on death, and search for ways to maximize the wealth you pass on. And once again you turn your attention to life insurance, this time permanent insurance.

There are many critics of life insurance who most often take a hard stand and suggest that the *only* life insurance you should ever consider is term insurance. They further maintain that life insurance is a bad investment. The truth is, neither term insurance nor permanent insurance is inherently good or bad, but if used in the wrong circumstances, both can lead to disaster.

Here's the simple lesson. Start by asking a simple

question: will someone I care about suffer financial consequences if I die? If yes, quantify those consequences and buy insurance for the appropriate amount using the most economical means possible – probably term insurance. If additional funds are available, and if it is your desire to transfer wealth to the next generation, then give consideration to permanent insurance. Over time, your insurance coverage will likely shift from term to permanent, or if wealth transfer is not important, from term insurance to no insurance at all. In essence, your first priority should be on the right amount of insurance for your needs. Secondary to that is the product type.

Putting the lesson to work

Let's examine life insurance more closely by looking at the role it plays at each phase in a typical life.

Life without dependents

First, we will step back into the first period of your life in which you are financially independent. You may be living alone, or you may be living with a spouse or partner, but you haven't yet taken on financial responsibilities for anyone else – most notably children. It's at this stage of your life that your life insurance needs are easy to understand. You don't need life insurance. You have no dependents. Even in a partnership or marriage, it will most often be assumed that each could survive financially without the other.

Some will make a case for buying insurance when you are young, arguing that it is cheaper, and more importantly, you should get insurance while you are healthy. Check out the rates for a 20 year old and a 30 year old and you may think paying for 10 years to get it cheaper isn't such a good idea. As for your health, there is always a risk that your health could change making it impossible to buy insurance, but the fact is this is rare until you hit middle age. You have to determine if this risk is worth the cost.

Probably your first foray into life insurance will be accompanied by the purchase of your first home. Even without financial dependents, life insurance is usually considered at this juncture because of the desire for lenders to minimize *their* risk. And if you purchase the home as a couple, it is quite possible that carrying the costs associated with the home without two incomes would be difficult. Life insurance would allow the surviving spouse to keep the home without sacrificing **lifestyle.**

Financial dependents

The most pressing need for insurance comes along with the first child. It is also at this point that life insurance may first appear complicated. Insuring the mortgage on the home was easy – there was a definite amount to be insured, and even a period of time to insure it (the mortgage term). Now the questions of how much and for how long are not so easily answered.

How much insurance *do* you need? The simplest way to answer this question is to break it into two parts. Lump sum needs and income needs.

Let's look at a specific example to illustrate how this can be done. Jake and Anna McKenzie have identified the following items as "lump sum" needs.

JAKE AND ANNA McKENZIE - LUMP SUM NEEDS	
Mortgage	$230,000
Credit card debt	$ 1,200
Line of credit	$ 5,200
Final expenses (funeral)	$ 10,000
Total lump sum needs	$246,400

Their current monthly expenses can be summarized as follows:

JAKE AND ANNA McKENZIE - MONTHLY EXPENSES	
Debt payments including mortgage	$1,750
RRSP savings for Jake	$1,000
RRSP savings for Anna	$ 800
General Living Expenses	$3,000
Total monthly expenses	**$6,550**

They have determined that in the event that Jake died, keeping in mind that they have allocated a lump sum to repay all debts, the family would need the following

ANNA McKENZIE - ONGOING NEEDS AFTER JAKE'S DEATH	
Debt payments including mortgage	$nil
RRSP savings for Jake	$nil
RRSP savings for Anna	$ 800
General Living Expenses	$2,300
Total monthly expenses	**$3,100**

Anna's net income after taxes and employee deductions is $2,500 per month. This means that she needs a supplement of $600 per month, (net of taxes) to stay in the same financial position. Let's assume that taxes will reduce her income by 25% meaning that the gross amount required becomes $800. A final factor to consider is inflation, and let's assume that would be 3%.

The McKenzies want to make sure that Anna has enough to support herself and the family while the children are dependent. After that, Anna can manage on her own financially, especially given she will be left with no debts and a home without a mortgage. They agree that providing Anna with income support then only needs to continue for 22 years, when their only child is expected to graduate from university.

Now, the question becomes, how much is needed to provide $800 per month, increasing by 3% per year, for 22 years? The answer to that is $165,590.

Now we simply add together the lump sum need of $246,400 and the income needs of $165,590 and we have our total life insurance need: $411,990.

We can go through the same exercise for Jake's needs in the event of Anna's death, and come up with the total insurance needs for the family. What's most important in working through this exercise is that you, and not the insurance advisor, become comfortable with the assumptions you are making. If they don't make sense to you, change them so that they do. This isn't an exact science – there's no right answer. This is a very personal matter and the level of protection you ultimately provide should reflect your own judgment. An advisor should simply give you the information, point out the differences created by changing the assumptions, and then let **you** decide.

Once you have determined the right amount of coverage, you must then decide on the right type. As already stated, there are only two types: term and permanent. But of course those types have sub-types that make things more confusing. Let's stop for a moment to look at product types now.

Term Insurance

Term insurance is almost always labeled with the duration of the term. For example ten-year term means that the premium is fixed for ten years. If the insurance is "renewable" (which term products usually are), then the policy can be renewed without re-qualifying at pre-set rates for another term. So after ten years the premium goes up and stays level for another ten-year term. Most term insurance is renewable to age 65 at least and usually to age 80 on this basis.

Ten-year term insurance is the best example as it is by far the most cost effective and sensible of the term products available today. You can also buy one-year, five-year, twenty-year and term-to-65 policies, but it's generally the ten-year term that represents the best value. Keep that in mind should an advisor push you towards something other than ten-year term.

Most term insurance products are also called "convertible," which means that prior to their expiry date, they can be converted to a permanent insurance plan offered by the same company. Given that term insurance is the product of choice while younger and permanent insurance is the right product as one gets older, this is a **valuable** benefit.

Permanent Insurance

The basis of permanent insurance is actually something known as term-to-100, which simply means the term of the contract with level premium is to age 100, with most insurers either paying out the death benefit or continuing the death benefit without requirement of additional premium when the insured reaches age 100.

Although term-to-100 does exist itself as a product, and did in fact enjoy a period of popularity, it has all but disappeared from the current marketplace. Most permanent plans today are either "whole life," which is the original permanent plan, or universal life, a more recent variation of the same.

The essence of both of these plans is that they combine a term-to-100 insurance contract with a savings or investment account. Within government imposed limits, money deposited into a permanent insurance policy in excess of the premium required to cover insurance costs can earn interest that is not subject to tax – making it a **tax-sheltered** investment.

The important difference between whole life and universal life is in the management of the investment portion of the contract. In a whole life contract, no investment decisions are required by the insured, but rather the investment return is based on the overall assets managed by the insurance company and returns are further smoothed out by averaging over many years. Thus the insured is relieved of the responsibility of making investment decisions and returns are much less volatile.

DO YOU WANT INSURANCE WITH THAT?

Whenever you obtain a mortgage, loan, or line of credit, you will likely also be offered an insurance package to pay the loan in the event of death, disability or critical illness. You will also receive offers in the mail from department stores, and credit card companies, offering protection on credit, as well as benefits on death, or disability. Decline them all. Linking your insurance to specific credit best serves the lender, not you. It isn't cheaper - in fact, usually it's more expensive.

This is piecemeal planning at its worst, and those who sign up for multiple coverages with low monthly costs end paying far too much for far too little protection. Arrange for all your life and disability insurance through one personal advisor and you will know that you have the right amount and type to do the job you want it to do.

Universal life came into existence during the 80s when impatient consumers wanted to take control of the investment portion in an attempt to generate superior returns. The product also better met the needs of consumers who found it difficult to forecast their ability to continue insurance premiums in the future. In universal life policies, the insurance costs and the investment account, (or cash value), are clearly delineated. Furthermore, the investment choices are in the hands of the insured, with choices ranging from guaranteed returns based on GIC rates to aggressive portfolios of equity funds.

Typically, permanent insurance - both universal life and whole life - are set up to follow one of three funding strategies.

First, they may be set up to be funded using the minimum premium for life. In other words, they are really nothing more than a term-to-100 policy, with no funds sitting in the cash value at all.

A second method is to determine the minimum amount of money in the cash account so that the income generated by those funds will pay the ongoing insurance costs. Once this level of funding is achieved, so long as the assumed rate of return is achieved, one could cease making contributions to the policy.

MEET BERT AND JULIE CALVIN

The most common problem for Canadians is that they are underinsured and don't know it. The reason? They have never really assessed what their needs are. Take for example Bert and Julie Calvin. Bert is an executive with a major Canadian consumer products company and accordingly has an excellent benefits plan, including five times his income in life insurance. That amounts to almost $750,000, and that seems like enough. Furthermore the company provides one times his income, ($150,000) on the life of Julie, and $10,000 on each of their three children. To many people, including Bert and Julie, that seems like more than enough. Our financial plan revealed otherwise.

Julie is a stay-at-home mom, and both Bert and Julie agreed that in the event that Bert died, they wanted Julie to be able to continue with their established lifestyle at least until the children completed their education. They had a wonderful lifestyle, with a price tag to match, and after accounting for the potential drop in expenses without Bert in the picture, they figured that the family would continue to need at least $5,000 per month. And that would be after paying off the mortgage, other loans and final expenses to the tune of $425,000. A quick calculation using inflation plus 2% as the return expected on life insurance proceeds, and we had the insurance need up to $1,500,000.

I am on record as stating that I dislike the proverbial "rule of thumb" whenever it is applied to financial planning, preferring to believe that each individual situation is unique and needs to be assessed on its own. But the rule of thumb for this particular situation may be worth noting. Where you are insuring a single bread winner in a young family the rule of thumb suggests that the amount of life insurance that is needed is ten times income. I am amazed at how often it is almost exactly the right answer.

Making some assumption for the interest rate earned on savings within the contract (which for universal life will also dictate investment style), it isn't too difficult to determine what this amount would be. For example, if the cost of insurance was $1,000 per year and the interest rate assumption was 5%, an account value of $20,000 would continue to pay the cost of insurance indefinitely. If you wanted to meet that $20,000 target in 8 years for example, you could deposit the $1,000 required premium each year, plus an additional $2,500 for those 8 years and you would have $20,000 plus whatever interest has accrued.

Anyhow, the response from the Calvins was initially disbelief and perhaps even suspicion that I was building a case to make a sale. And so we toyed with different scenarios. We considered a higher rate of return, but when Julie considered the investment strategy she would need to stick to in order to achieve it, she wondered if 2% above inflation was in fact too high. We considered the possibility that Julie would go back to work, but that idea was vetoed by Calvin.

As they pondered this issue, I pointed out that this was something they didn't have to do, I was merely pointing out what needed to be done if it was in fact their wish that the family would remain in a similar financial position should the worst happen. And I suggested that they look at the cost of getting what they wanted before they looked for ways to avoid it.

To add $750,000 of ten year term life insurance on Bert's life carried a monthly premium of less than $50. Bert's words exactly, "That's nothing!"

They proceeded with the insurance and in fact after another discussion about the financial implications of losing Julie, they added $150,000 on her life as well.

It's easy to get caught up living an extraordinary life and forget that despite our best intentions, there are still risks ahead that could turn that life upside down. The Calvins perfectly illustrate the best advice one could receive in this area. Properly identify and quantify the loss associated with the risk. Determine the cost involved in passing this risk to an insurer. Then, based on having all the facts, make a decision. It's simple, really.

Finally, an individual may want to take maximum advantage of the tax sheltering opportunity afforded permanent insurance by Canada Revenue Agency (CRA). In this case, the maximum allowable deposits will be made each year, (as determined by CRA), thus building up the account value to its absolute maximum level. This method is known as "maximum funding."

Getting back to our example, what type of insurance is right for Jake and Anna? Both of them agree that at some point they will want to pay attention to their estate, and ideally they want to leave funds for the benefit of their children, (and one day perhaps grandchildren). But at the moment, given the costs of carrying the house, a child and trying to save for their future, there isn't much room in their budget for anything else. In other words, they are looking for a low-cost solution, but would like to retain the right to change to the long term product when cash flow permits. Like most young couples, the right solution is ten-year term that is convertible to permanent insurance.

Empty nest and estate planning

As children grow up and eventually move out on their own, most parents come to realize that they are going to have a lot more cash on their hands. The life insurance that was protecting the family now appears to be redundant. But at the same time, assets are beginning to grow. Protection needs have disappeared, but estate planning questions are probably emerging.

As we become more aware of our own mortality, we start to consider how our assets will be distributed when we are gone, and we start to worry about the erosion that is inevitably caused by taxes and other costs of settling our estate.

The first thing to do is to ensure that wills are up to date. Wills shouldn't be left to this stage of life of course; they should be put in place as soon as there are assets to distribute, even if all of the assets would simply go to a spouse or immediate family. But at this stage, they should be updated and possibly altered to take advantage of any opportunities to minimize tax and probate. Consult your lawyer for the appropriate advice.

Next, you should run through a simple "what-if" scenario to see what will happen to your assets – based on your current will and beneficiary designations - and investigate any opportunities to make changes to increase the value of the assets left behind. Let's look at another example to highlight the key items to consider.
Charlie and Edna Wilkinson are both 60. They have four grown children and five grandchildren (so far!) They have no debts, and the following assets:

CHARLIE AND EDNA WILKINSON - ASSET INVENTORY

House (joint)	$250,000
Charlie's RRSP	$300,000
Edna's RRSP	$200,000
Non-registered portfolio (joint)	$475,000
Bank balance (joint)	$15,000
Total assets	**$1,240,000**

There are two things to consider when examining the value of assets when one dies: taxes and probate. Under Canadian tax law, when the first of either Charlie or Edna dies, all assets will flow to the remaining spouse without tax consequence. This is known as a "spousal rollover." This provision is not available to any other beneficiaries, including children, and so taxes and probate are really only an issue on the final death.

Let's examine the list of assets again and assign estimates regarding taxes and probate for their joint estate (that is, on the final death).

CHARLIE AND EDNA WILKINSON - ESTATE OVERVIEW

	Current value	Tax (estimate)	Probate (estimate)	Net to estate
House (joint)	$250,000	$nil	$3,350	$246,750
Charlie's RRSP	$300,000	$138,000	$4,500	$157,500
Edna's RRSP	$200,000	$92,000	$3,000	$78,000
Non-registered portfolio (joint)*	$475,000	$40,250	$7125	$426,600
Bank balance (joint)	$15,000	$nil	$225	$14,775
Total assets	**$1,240,000**	**$270,250**	**$18,200**	**$923,625**

* cost base of $300,000

(Note: This table assumes a tax rate of 46% and probate of $250 on the first $50,000 and $15 per thousand thereafter, based on present Ontario laws. Each province varies slightly, although all follow a similar pattern.)

MEET MARTY JAMESON

Despite what insurance companies and agents might tell you, it is possible to have too much insurance. And that can be a serious financial mistake.

Marty Jameson is a 68-year old man whose wife died 8 years ago. He is the parent of grown children; Martin Junior is 28 and lives alone, and Susie is 32 and married with 2 children of her own. Marty is well organized financially and was quickly able to provide a balance sheet and a complete list of expenses. His well-founded concern was a fear that he may outlive his money and ultimately place a financial burden on his children.

As a self-employed contractor all his life, Marty doesn't have a pension plan, and so his income is derived from his government benefits and his withdrawals from his RRIF and non-registered savings. Marty calculated that since his savings were depleting already, he figured they would run out unless he was unfortunate enough not to enjoy a long life. We put together a financial plan and it was clear to see that Marty was correct.

There are always many things to consider when confronted with this scenario – increasing rates of return, reducing expenses, taking equity from the house, etc. But there was something in his financial picture that didn't seem to fit. He had a $500,000 permanent life insurance policy with an annual premium of almost $15,000 payable for life. The policy had been purchased only 4 years prior.

I questioned the reasons for this policy and instead of answering directly he quickly said, "I don't want to cancel the life insurance," as if it was a topic not to be discussed. I persisted.

As you can see, if nothing else changes, a total of $288,450 will be paid in taxes and probate. Naturally, Charlie and Edna want to know what, if anything, can be done to reduce their liability.

First of all, we need to look at asset values at future points, especially out near life expectancy. This is best done in the context of a financial plan. In the case of Charlie and Edna, it is anticipated that most of the figures will initially rise. However, as inflation pushes their expenses beyond their earnings – estimated to be in about 11

Of course his intentions were wonderful. He wanted to be sure that his children each received an amount that would make a difference. He wanted them to pay off their mortgages, help their own children through school and get out from under the financial pressures that he knew they were experiencing. The only problem was, he was now starting to feel some serious financial pressure himself.

An assessment of his estate suggested that if he died today, after taxes and final expenses, Martin and Susie would divide about $800,000. Add in the insurance, and that number topped $1,300,000.

I presented Marty with another financial plan, and did what many agents would consider unthinkable; I recommended that Marty reduce the insurance to $100,000, thereby freeing up almost $1,000 per month in cash flow. Not surprisingly this plan put Marty on much better financial footing. The problem was, the projected value of the estate at life expectancy was now down to a mere $350,000, and if he lived longer it continued to decline, hitting bottom of course at $100,000. In Marty's words, "Given inflation, that might not be enough to bury me in 25 years. It's certainly not going to help the kids the way I want to."

Marty had to make a tough choice. Ultimately, he had to find the balance between helping his children someday and helping them today, (by helping himself). After some thinking, Marty decided to reduce his insurance, although not to my recommended level. A comment Marty made neatly sums up the proper approach to insurance planning. "I know what to do because I know the amount of insurance that makes sense. I need to buy what I can afford, given that my plan is to live a long and happy life and a not short and miserable one."

years – the values will begin to fall. The financial plan shows their tax liability will simply rise and fall, peaking at just over $400,000 and never falling below $200,000.

There are a number of things that Charlie and Edna could do to reduce this liability, such as creating a family trust, giving the children part or whole ownership of certain assets now, or spending RRSP assets more quickly in an effort to reduce the tax liability on death. The problem with all of these is that they simply move the tax liability from death to today. The taxes can't be avoided, only delayed, and any accountant will tell you that delaying the payment of tax is generally **a good thing.**

Here are some other alternatives:

1. Consider moving the RRSP assets to an insurance company, either in the form of segregated funds, or fixed income products. A beneficiary can be named directly (the children will be named secondary to a surviving spouse), and these assets will then bypass their will and not be subject to probate. This would reduce probate fees by $7,500.

2. The same should be considered for non-registered assets. However, selling these assets now would trigger the tax liability of $40,250 in an attempt to save $7,125 in probate. For Charlie and Edna at least, it's not a good idea.

3. Buy life insurance to offset some of the taxes owing on the death of the second spouse.

A joint-and-last-to-die life insurance policy in the amount of $250,000 for Charlie and Edna has a premium of $2,961. If they allocated $9,354 each year over the next 5 years, the account value using a return of 6% would be $39,627. This would carry the policy costs indefinitely. This gives their estate an initial lift of $250,000. If you compare this strategy with the strategy of leaving the $9,354 invested outside an insurance contract, even at age 90 the insurance provides a greater value to the estate, and much more certainty.

Charlie and Edna purchase the insurance and make the small changes to their portfolio, and reduce their projected estate loss to almost nil. In the end, this was far less complicated than they expected it to be. And they are excited by the fact that the financial plan has not only put to rest their concerns that their estate may be decimated, but also by the fact that in the process of investigating this issue we created a financial plan that shows they are going to have considerable wealth as long as they live and further that they will leave behind considerable wealth for children and grandchildren.

MAKING THE SIMPLE COMPLEX

Taking the simple idea of life insurance and making it a complicated product is not a recent phenomenon. Consider the comments from the *Eleventh Annual Report of the Superintendent of the Insurance Department of the State of New York*, April 1, 1870.

"As already intimated, it is believed to be a fact, now causing quite general complaint, that there are too many complicated schemes or plans of insuring, and conducting companies, as well as too many and too elaborate forms of contract or policy. Each new company announces some new feature in its business, which is to enure greatly to the advantage of the insured, and thus, with some seventy different companies, each urging their superiority over all others, he who seeks insurance, if he stops to hear all the arguments, and deliberately determine which is really the best company, is likely to die before he reaches a conclusion."

This is the complete journey of life insurance in a typical life. From protecting the financial security of those of you look after, to ensuring that your hard-earned assets make the journey intact to children and grandchildren. It's not so much about making your life extraordinary as it is making sure that the lives of others are extraordinary when you're gone. The greatest wealth is the ability to give. And life insurance is best understood when it is seen **as a gift.**

SIMPLE MONEY

Young single people don't need life insurance.

People married with no children should consider insuring their mortgage.

People with children should insure breadwinners to allow the family to maintain lifestyle.

The tax preferred status of life insurance makes it an unbeatable investment from an estate planning perspective.

Life insurance can be used to enhance the wealth of beneficiaries.

EXTRAORDINARY LIFE

Life insurance is about giving to others to help make their lives extraordinary.

Disability income and Critical illness insurance

Not all of life's events fall within our control. The only thing we can reasonably do is assess the risk ahead of us and take what measures exist to protect against potential losses.

A brief historical perspective

The introduction of accident and sickness benefits didn't take place until the late 1800s, making these policies relative newcomers in the world of insurance. Not surprisingly, true disability income (DI) contracts like those in use today were initially offered by fraternal organizations in the U.S. and thus, like life insurance, have a history that mixes business with benevolence. But the history of this industry suggests this is a difficult product to make into a profitable business.

Throughout the 1900s, the disability business grew with an increased number of insurers vying for the attention of workers looking to protect their all-important income. In an effort to attract market share, companies modified contract language to broaden the scope of coverage, a trend that would continue to the late 1980s. Of course changes made to contracts attracted new business - and increased claims, sometimes in the wrong proportion.

Whereas life insurance is based on fairly predictable statistics of life expectancy, disability insurers have limited data upon which to base underwriting decisions, and are faced with many issues that are of little relevance to life insurers. The main difference of course is that death is almost always easily verified, whereas disability is seldom so straightforward. Particularly as the pattern of claims has shifted into the areas of mental and nervous disorders, insurers have been faced with the task of determining the legitimacy of claims. Over the past decade this same trend has led to a retrenching of product language and a focus on profitability instead of volume of sales.

An even more recent entry to the insurance marketplace is critical illness insurance, (CI). Developed in South Africa in the early 1980s, this product quickly spread to other developed countries including Canada and the U.S. Where DI provides an ongoing income stream when working income is interrupted by an accident or sickness, CI provides a lump sum benefit at the onset of an insured condition, most notably, cancer, heart disease or stroke. The idea was introduced by Dr. Marius Barnaard (brother to the famous heart surgeon) who noted that patients who previously would not have survived heart attacks were suddenly facing new expenses that were causing serious financial hardship.

While growth in some parts of the world has been fairly rapid, Canadians have been slower to accept CI, no doubt due in part to our government sponsored medical plan. Still, insurers are continuing to fine tune this product; they believe that with the aging of the baby boomers and the continuing high incidence of cancer and heart disease, it is reasonable to expect steady growth ahead.

The simple lesson

Disability income insurance

When you start working sometime in your 20s, the statistics show that there is about a 50% chance that you will suffer at least one disability lasting 90 days or longer before you retire. For most people, the idea of being without a pay cheque for 90 days leads to thoughts of bankruptcy. The possibility that a disability may leave you unable to work for many years, even a lifetime, is almost inconceivable.

The need for DI is exactly the same as the need for life insurance. In both instances income stops and those who depend on that income may face financial hardship. The main difference of course is that if you are disabled, you are among those in trouble. The same financial suffering occurs, but you get to stick around and see just how **bad** it **gets.**

This isn't a pleasant topic. An accident or a serious illness is rarely a planned event on the path through an extraordinary life. But not all of life's events fall within our control. The only thing we can reasonably do is assess the risk ahead of us and take what measures exist to protect against potential losses. Disability is one of those risks. And DI is the reasonable source of protection.

Critical illness insurance

This is not a replacement for DI. CI pays a lump sum at the onset of specific diseases, called "covered conditions." DI pays when you have a loss of income due to a disability, regardless of what condition caused the disability, and ideally keeps paying an income until you return to work.

The bottom line on CI is this: those who feel the greatest need for this kind of protection often can't afford it after paying for life insurance, and disability insurance, not to mention a mortgage, the monthly bills, and saving for the future. And, well, those things are in fact, more important. On the other hand, if money is no object, well, you may **not** really **need** it.

You may of course land somewhere in the middle, and if so, this can be valuable protection. But be careful. The teary-eyed stories used to sell this product are very compelling.

Putting the lessons to work

Thinking about disability insurance follows the same process as most other financial issues. Start by determining where you are now – what benefits do you have already? Then determine what you would like to have. Finally, put whatever plans are needed in place to fill the gap.

There are several problems associated with this rather simple process. First, most people don't know what disability protection they have, or even if they have any. Second, they don't know what is reasonable to assume they should have. And finally, getting good help is hard – very few financial advisors have a reasonable level of expertise in this area, often ignoring the subject altogether thus leaving their clients to assume that it is unimportant and therefore often under-protected.

Let's look then at the basic building blocks of disability insurance and provide you with enough information to examine your own situation and ask **intelligent** questions.

Benefit amount

If you become disabled and you can't work, how much money will you receive each month? It's surprising how many people don't know the answer to that question. In fact, most people aren't even sure where to go to get the answer.

For many Canadians, DI is often a key part of employer-sponsored benefits. Usually it comes in two forms: short term disability (STD) which covers the first several months, followed by long term disability (LTD) which takes over and continues until the claim ends, or age 65, whichever comes first. It is partly due to the prevalence of group plans that DI is so poorly understood. The average employee thinks, "If I'm sick and can't work, my company will keep paying me," and that's all they think they need to know. For the most part, this blind faith may be forgiven. However, lying in a hospital bed reading the terms and conditions of your group insurance may be a bad time to find out it's **less than you expected.**

DIFFERENT PREMIUMS FOR DISABILITY INSURANCE

Life insurance premiums are generally higher for men than women of the same age. That's because women tend to outlive men. When it comes to disability insurance the tables are turned - women pay the higher premium. The logic is the same: women collect more claim dollars. For both sexes, over the past several decades we are living longer, and we are disabled more frequently. The result of these trends has been a gradual lowering of life insurance rates and gradually increasing DI rates.

In the case of group plans, benefit amounts are usually based on a percentage of working income. For example, many plans will pay 66.6% of base salary. This form of insurance is known as "reimbursing," as the benefit is based on the income level at the time of the disability. Group plans then will grow along with your income, until they hit any cap or ceiling that may be imposed.

Individual or privately-owned disability insurance contracts pay a specific face amount and are thus known as "indemnifying." These plans don't automatically grow with your income, and therefore must be maintained by reviewing and changing as necessary to keep insurance levels appropriate.

Most disability insurance contracts are set up to pay benefits that are non-taxable. In the case of group plans then the 66.6% benefit level (which is based on gross salary) is probably closer to 85% or more of net take home pay. When contracts are established this way, the premium must be paid by the insured in after-tax dollars. Many employees express unhappiness in the fact that disability insurance premiums are not paid for by the employer, especially in light of the fact that everything else generally is. In fact, this is a good thing - it means the plan was carefully constructed.

Almost all individual plans, since premiums are paid by the insured and are not considered tax deductible, will pay **non-taxable** income during a disability.

How much coverage should you have? Most agents will tell you "all you can get." While it's true that a disabled individual will never say they have too much income from the insurance company, it is also true that one needs to balance the desire for protection with prudent use of current funds. The simplest approach is to first determine how much money you need on a monthly basis in order to survive financially. That will then set the minimum level you are looking for. Then determine how much is actually available from insurers.

You may find that your minimum number is already higher than the amount you can get. This is because insurers have learned the hard way that providing too much income at the time of disability can have a dramatically bad effect on claims and hence profitability. The fact is: if claimants are receiving sufficient income from disability plans to keep them comfortable in their current lifestyle, the incentive to return to work is reduced, and a larger percentage of claimants will stay on claim for longer periods of time. For this reason, insurers are careful not to provide too much coverage. And they give careful consideration to other disability insurance benefits already in place.

Definition of disability

The second question to ask when examining disability insurance is: "how do I qualify for benefits?" The obvious answer is: "when you are disabled." The problem is, different contracts have different ways of defining "disability."

It may appear that there are countless ways to define disability, and sales people are notorious for pushing the use of one word vs. another in various aspects of contract language. In fact, there are only two ways to describe a disability. The first is to consider the insured disabled when they are unable to work in their own occupation. If, for example, an electrician loses the use of his hands and is therefore unable to continue working, the insurance company will consider that individual disabled and will not have the right to coerce him into some other occupation. This is commonly referred to as "own occupation" or "regular occupation."

The other method of defining disability is called "any occupation," and as the name suggests in this scenario the electrician would only be considered disabled if he was unable to do any job that was considered reasonable. This of course gives the insurance company much more latitude to push claimants back to work.

Many contracts, (particularly group plans) include both definitions, usually defining disability as "own occupation" for the first two years, and then considering the disability to continue beyond that point only if the insured meets the more stringent "any occupation" test. Which definition you should have in your plan depends on what you can get, and how much you are willing to pay for disability insurance.

Some contracts may further distinguish between a total disability, (basic to most contracts) and a partial (or residual) disability; an additional feature of some contracts. While the definition of total disability is the subject of much debate,

GOVERNMENT-SPONSORED DISABILITY INSURANCE?

There are government benefits available to disabled persons under the Canada Pension Plan, but they are fairly limited (maximum benefits are in the range of $1,000 per month) and few recipients actually qualify for the maximum amount. The other problem with the CPP disability benefit is that the government defines disability as "severe and prolonged." In practice this means being en route to the grave. When planning your disability benefits you should do what individual disability insurance companies do – ignore the CPP.

the definition of partial disability is even more so. For the most part, a partial disability will be defined as a situation in which you are unable to work full time in your regular occupation, but you are in fact able to work part of the time or full time but with limited capacity either in your own occupation or another occupation. This can in many instances prove to be a **very important benefit** for both the insured and the insurer.

If our electrician for example decides that he wants to work, he may unfortunately find going to back to work an unattractive option if he can't work as many hours or as effectively as he did prior to the disability. If going back to work means less pay and a stoppage in claim cheques, he may decide the better thing to do is stay home. This really isn't beneficial to either party. Many insurers of course would be willing to negotiate at this point, and most group plans would attempt to include this under contract language that deals with "rehabilitation." For the security of the insured, however, nothing beats having it spelled out in **black** and **white.** Look for contracts that specifically deal with partial disabilities if possible.

Benefit period

If you are disabled for a long period - perhaps even indefinitely - how long can you count on your benefits? The most common duration is to age 65 (and for most group plans this would be the case). Some individual plans, however, will be arranged to pay for shorter durations, often two, three or five years. Sometimes this is a limit imposed by the insurer and is a way for them to offer coverage to occupation classes or specific individuals whom they deem to be higher risks. Occasionally the contract is arranged this way by the insured as a way to reduce premium. It is tempting for instance to elect a shorter benefit period and also a shorter waiting period (see next section) in order to increase the probability of making a claim. It is much more likely you will suffer a disability of a few weeks as opposed to several years. This is gambling, not insuring. Keep this rule in mind: insure the things you can't replace or recover from on your own. We insure our houses from total destruction. But if a window breaks, we replace it on our own. Since a long term or permanent disability would be the most devastating, one should always elect to obtain benefits to age 65, or as long as the insurer will offer.

Waiting period

For most group plans, benefits normally begin at day one of a disability in the case of an accident, and after one or two weeks in the case of a sickness. Even in the absence of a short term disability plan, most employers have a sick day policy that would allow an employee to miss a period of days or weeks without an interruption in pay, and usually for longer periods long term disability plans are in place to **take over.**

In the case of individual plans, a waiting period, (sometimes called an elimination period) is established in the contract; usually the shortest available is 30 days, and the most popular is 90 days. Think of this as a period of "self-insurance," like a deductible on a car insurance policy. There is a dramatic drop in premium when one moves from 30 days to 60 days and from 60 days to 90 days as you are removing the risk of short term claims from the insurer. Extending the waiting period to 120 days or 180 days has a less dramatic effect on premium. For that reason, 90 days has become **the waiting period of choice.**

For those who are eligible for government sponsored Employment Insurance (EI), often 120 days is the better choice, or the choice required by insurers as EI benefits are available to be paid up to the 120th day of a disability.

Cost of living

Inflation is always an enemy to consider when creating any long term financial plan. In the case of disability insurance, the question to answer is: will my benefit amount **increase** over time?

What you should look for is a "cost of living adjustment" benefit, or COLA. Most plans that include a COLA clause will adjust benefits paid each year to a claimant by a fixed amount (in individual plans often 2% to 4%), or based on changes to the consumer price index (CPI). Some will cap CPI increases on an annual or a cumulative basis. The important thing isn't so much how it's increased as the fact that it is increased. Without an increasing benefit, what you really have is a decreasing benefit since the cost of whatever you are buying eats up an increasing portion of your income each year.

The second item to consider is the ability to increase your benefit amount prior to a claim. In the case of group plans that automatically adjust to match your income, this is taken care of, but in the case of individual plans, this is left to the insured. Most individual plans offer "future earnings protection" or some similar benefit. This provides the insured with an option to increase coverage every year on the policy anniversary in an effort to keep pace with inflation. This is a **very valuable benefit**, since disability insurance is not always easy to obtain. Small changes in your health can have disastrous consequences to your ability to buy disability insurance. The option to purchase each year without medical underwriting can make the difference between having the right level of insurance and continually falling behind as income levels rise.

Exclusions

More important perhaps than determining what is covered is determining what

NON-CANCELLABLE INSURANCE

The standard form of the DI contract is "non-cancellable and guaranteed continuable" (non-can). Simply stated, this means that the insurance company does not have the right to cancel your coverage or change it in any detrimental way; they must continue the coverage during the life of the contract (usually to age 65) at the stated premium level. Recently, insurance companies have wondered about the practicality of this one-way street and began offering "guaranteed renewable" contracts which give the insurer the right to change the contract or the premium so long as they change them for all insureds in the same occupation class at the same time. At this point, the non-can contract remains king, and if available, it's the best option for most people.

isn't covered. Most contracts contain a list of exclusions that in all cases will include normal pregnancy (which otherwise would meet most definitions of disability) and an act of war. From there, the list will depend on the individual policy, and may include such things as: self-inflicted injuries, participation in a criminal act, travel outside the country, mental or nervous disorders, and participation in a riot. Sometimes these items will appear to be innocuous, but they are all there for the same reason – to limit the liability of the insurer and therefore push more of the risk back to you. Your goal is to keep the list as short as possible, while still keeping the premiums within your budget.

Also of note in most insurance contracts is the handling of pre-existing conditions. If you have a medical history that includes issues that could turn into potential claims, the insurer will likely want to reduce their exposure to what may clearly be a higher risk of claim. Group plans generally throw a blanket over this and simply exclude all claims that arise from a condition that pre-existed within the two years prior to joining the plan.

In the case of individual policies, the insurer most often uses specific exclusions to eliminate coverage for pre-existing conditions, even if the insured has fully recovered. In some cases, they may even decline to provide any coverage at all. When this occurs invariably the insured responds negatively, feeling that perhaps they are being "discriminated" against unfairly. The truth is, without the ability for the insurer to actively select who they will insure and under what terms, the whole notion of insurance as a business would be difficult to contemplate. If you find yourself considering a policy that doesn't match your expectations, in almost all cases the right thing for you to do is to accept the policy anyway. You may wish to consider searching for coverage from another insurer, but in most cases you will find that due to the high risk nature of the business, most insurers are similarly conservative and seldom will they try to win business on the basis of making more aggressive underwriting decisions.

Return of premium

Disability insurance shares a trait with many other forms of insurance that make them a "hate-to-but-have-to" kind of purchase; the insured buys the insurance hoping that the premiums turn out to be a total waste of money. A neat response to this problem is the idea of return of premium.

Return of premium (ROP) is a benefit that some insurers will attach to an individual DI policy. It first appeared in Canada in the 80s when disability insurance companies were aggressively competing for market share.

The concept is **simple.** The insurance company collects the premium to cover the risk, plus an additional premium to invest. If the insured has no claims during a prescribed number of years (or at termination of the policy) then the insurance company will pay the insured a sum equal to a portion of or all of the premiums paid. In other words, if you don't use the benefit, we'll give you your money back. It sounds fantastic, even more so when you examine the potential return on your extra premium. But, closer examination may limit some of the initial appeal.

The first thing to do is to simply calculate the rate of return you might experience if you purchased this plan and didn't make a claim. For example, Norm, a 40 year old non-smoker and an office worker buys disability insurance from Great West Life. His premium is $58.88 per month for $2,000 per month of base coverage with a 90 day waiting period and benefits payable to age 65. He can add ROP for $11.71 per month and under the terms of the contract would be entitled to receive 50% of the total premiums paid on termination of the contract, no sooner than age 55. So if Norm has no claims at age 55 he can surrender the contract and he will receive $6,353.10 ($70.59 x 12 months x 15 years x 50%). Considering he paid an additional $11.71 each month to attract that refund, the return on that monthly extra is 13.6%. So far it's looking very good. The catch is that the return of premium amount will be reduced by the any claim amount

ACCIDENT AND SICKNESS: THERE IS A DIFFERENCE

If possible, make sure your policy covers both accident and sickness. Most do of course, but accident-only policies often look very attractive due to their low premiums (and correspondingly low claim payouts).

Norm is paid during that 15 year period. Based on a monthly benefit of $2,000, a claim of 3.2 months ($6,353.10 / $2,000) would completely wipe out his refund. That's a disability of 6.2 months given Norm's 90 day waiting period.

Is this a good bet?

And there it is. The problem with the ROP rider is that it turns an insurance contract into a bet, and in doing so often turns a claimant into a non-claimant. Imagine sitting at home recovering from an auto accident. You are expected to recover and be back to work in 5 or 6 months. Do you file a claim and risk losing your return of premium? What if you don't file and you're unable to return to work when expected? What if you don't file and you have another disability claim in the future?

It is a fact that products that contain the ROP rider have fewer short term claims. **Go figure.** This is calculated in the return rate they are able to offer on the extra premium. In the end, the insurance companies make just as much money (sometimes more) when ROP is included. So who is losing out?

ROP is also available on CI contracts and in that case, it might make more sense. Most of the ROP riders on CI come with a 100% return of premium on

DISABILITY INSURANCE ≠ WORKER'S COMPENSATION

For many Canadians, disability insurance is synonymous with the Worker's Compensation Board (in Ontario known as the Worker's Safety and Insurance Board). The legislation that operates these benefits has two components. First, benefits are provided to employees who are disabled due to work-related accidents or illnesses. Second, the legislation eliminates the right of the disabled employee to sue the employer for damages. Worker's compensation is required for many industries, particularly those involving labourers such as construction and manufacturing. It is noteworthy that only a small percentage of the claim dollars paid out by disability insurers are due to work-related accidents. The vast majority in fact are due to illness, and this is especially true as individuals get older. So, Worker's Comp certainly doesn't negate the need to consider additional DI; in fact, if it isn't mandatory, it may be best to replace it entirely. If your employer is paying for Worker's Comp that may be good news for them and you, as often much more comprehensive coverage can be installed for a lower premium.

cancellation of the policy, a refund that is forfeited if a claim is made. The difference here is that CI is an "all or nothing" type contract. If you have a claim the cheque you receive should easily exceed the potential ROP claim and so you won't find yourself crunching numbers to decide.

Other options

There are many other features that can be added to plans to make them much more expensive than they need to be. Examples include short waiting periods, lifetime benefit periods, first day benefits for accidents or hospitalization, contributions to savings while disabled, and benefits that continue at 100% while working in another occupation. Some of these would be nice to have, but none are essential. Remember: the goal is to spend **the least** to get **the most.**

DI Essentials

A good disability insurance contract will offer the following, in this order:

1. The right monthly benefit – what you need to survive at least.
2. Benefits payable to age 65, or for the longest period an insurer will provide up to age 65.
3. Minimal exclusions, especially those that concern you, but in the end, take the best you can get.
4. Protection against inflation.
5. Coverage for partial disabilities if it is available at a reasonable cost.

The **bottom line** on DI is this: if you don't have any, get some. If you do have coverage, determine how much you have, and the quality of the coverage based on the items discussed here. If necessary, "top-up" your current group coverage with a personal plan to get the protection you want. Get help from an agent with experience and expertise in this area to plug any holes. Then put the contract in a drawer and hope that you forget about it, except for once a year when the insurer will remind you to increase the coverage to match earnings.

MEET RICK AND TINA ELLIOT

Sometimes our emotions can lead us astray. We all know this is true in the world of investing, but it's equally true in the world of insurance.

Rick and Tina Elliot had their first child, Rachel, a few years ago, and in a period of overwhelming emotion, the couple got carried away with protecting their precious bundle of joy. Rick is a site foreman with a contracting firm and because his job involves a hard hat and safety shoes he has a reminder each day of the risks he is taking. Tina was an employee at the local bank, but they decided when Rachel was born that Tina's place was at home. Both have made several sacrifices in order to manage the financial consequences of living on Rick's income alone.

For the first year of Rachel's life Rick and Tina were an insurance company's dream come true. Every time they received an offer in the mail to protect a member of the family they accepted. By the end of the year, they had 8 different insurance contracts with various banks and insurance companies ranging from life insurance on their line of credit to hospital benefits to critical illness. Despite spending nearly $200 per month for all of these various benefits, they felt at risk. That's not surprising given that they really couldn't say what insurance they had, or what they needed.

We did the usual analysis to determine life insurance needs and determined exactly how much would be required by surviving family members should either Rick or Tina - or heaven forbid both - die prematurely. It turned out that insurance to cover that could be arranged for $39.56 per month.

Then we turned to DI. The family was currently living on about $3,000 per month, but based on Rick's gross income of $50,000 the most DI they could obtain was $2,600 per month. That made the "how much coverage should we have" question easy to answer, but left them uneasy about that $400 per month gap. An appropriately structured DI policy (90 day wait, to age 65 benefits, COLA, future income protection and partial benefits) had a premium of $109 per month. This seemed like a lot of course, especially compared to the relatively low life insurance premium. But I pointed out that disability was a much greater risk, and furthermore, a long term claim could easily pay out more than the life insurance sum (which was $500,000 for Rick).

When we examined the other insurance contracts they had arranged, all were discarded. For the most part, these contracts were either simply not valuable, (such as the hospital indemnity plan that paid $100 per day for hospital stays longer than 5 days), or too expensive relative to the coverage we were considering on a consolidated basis, (one of the life policies carried a premium of about half the cost of the policy we set up but provided only one tenth of the coverage).

The net result then was a drop in monthly premiums from $200 to under $150. With the extra $50 in mind we returned to another insurance plan that had been seriously considered: critical illness. I wondered if I was doing a disservice to this very conscientious young family not to make a stronger case for CI, especially in light of the fact that a small amount of CI already in force was being discarded.

Common sense began to take charge. Tina summed it up in admirable fashion. "We want to make sure that if anything happens to Rick or myself we can survive financially. After that, we need to save for Rachel's education, pay off our mortgage and ultimately save for our own retirement. Things are already tight. The extra $50, in my opinion, has more important things to do than buy more insurance. That's just my opinion." Rick nodded in agreement; apparently it was his opinion also.

They both looked at me, probably expecting, some sales-speak that might convince them otherwise. But I just reassured them and said, "Insurance should do two things. First, it must be there if needed, and when called upon it must do what you expect it to do. I'm confident the plans you have in place now will do that. Second, it should provide peace of mind at all times. It won't do that if you are constantly doubting your decision and wondering if you are paying too much or worse, paying for something you really don't need. I think we have reached the point of equilibrium on these two things."

Next on the agenda for Tina and Rick were much more inspiring things, like planning their lives with Rachel. With the peace of mind issue resolved, their minds were suddenly clear and the road ahead was paved with a greater certainty of many wonderful years.

Critical illness

The intent of insurance when applied correctly is to replace for a loss. If you total your car, insurance helps you buy a new car. If your house burns down, insurance helps you rebuild it. If you lose your income, insurance replaces it. These all make sense, and for the most part are necessary products based on our shared values. Critical illness is a departure from this in that it provides money whether or not an actual loss occurs. So instead of being true insurance, **critical illness is best understood as a distorted lottery** – one that admittedly most people don't want to win but fear they will.

At the onset of a heart attack, or cancer, or a stroke, or any of the listed covered conditions in a CI contract, you may experience a loss of income. Or you may need funds to obtain additional medical help not covered by government plans. Either of these situations would constitute a real need for insurance. (Important to note of course is that the possibility of lost income should be covered with disability insurance). So the "insurance" aspect of CI boils down to covering expenses not otherwise handled by government medical plans. That being the case, the questions to raise are: how often does this occur? And, what is the price tag of the possible needs?

The answer to the first question at the moment is, not very often. While most of us have been touched in some way by heart disease, stroke or cancer, not many of us have encountered situations in which friends or loved ones have experienced financial hardship, or worse, were unable to receive proper treatment due to limitations in existing programs. More often it's the loss of earnings that is the cause of financial problems, and that is a DI issue. This of course could all change if Canada adopts a "two-tier" medical system – allowing those with money to step to the front of the line, or receive preferred treatment. And at this time a "two-tier" system does appear to be a real possibility.

Even more difficult to assess is the potential cost of these services. We have all heard the horror stories of the cost of medical treatment in the U.S. Accordingly, we are well advised to never leave Canada without appropriate travel insurance for medical care. So it's not difficult to imagine that a sum - sufficient to allow us to travel to a U.S. destination and receive the medical attention we need for our covered disease - will be in the tens or possibly hundreds of thousands of dollars. Just the same, at the onset of any one of the covered conditions, you may find that you quickly recover, return to work and experience no out of pocket expense. The range as you can see is enormous.

CI would make **more sense** if you paid a premium and were subsequently entitled to get the services you need if and when you need them. But it's not designed that way. Instead, regardless of your actual need, you simply get a lump sum of cash that you predetermined which is almost certain to be too high or too low.

It is certainly true that when stricken by cancer, a heart attack, etc, most people will find plenty of things they want to do that will put the additional money to good use. Take time off from work, spend more time with family, travel, and particularly if the disease is terminal, experience the things that otherwise would go on the "I wish I had" list.

Furthermore, the sudden onset of a covered illness usually comes with a very significant emotional impact. Even though appropriate disability insurance might be in place (as it should), even the best DI plans will provide less than 100% of prior income. The reduced cash flow will simply add one more stress to an already stressful situation. So, CI benefits in most cases will aid in the emotional recovery of the "critically ill" person, and his or her family. This is perhaps the best argument of all for a substantial lump sum of cash to suddenly appear at this moment.

So what should you do? First, make sure that DI needs are taken care of, and don't expect CI to cover that problem. Then, if you are concerned about a major disease striking, (and many naturally will be) then purchase an appropriate sum of CI to provide additional protection while still fitting into your overall budget.

Again, insurance planning is really about establishing priorities. In order to put the risks you face in perspective along with the other items that call on your resources, you need to understand those risks. A planner or an agent may push you to consider a risk that you would prefer to avoid thinking about, and you may get to thinking that if you bought all the insurance that was recommended, you may become "insurance poor." Don't let that natural reaction stop you from doing the important work here, and that is assessing the risks and making decisions based on all available information.

Should you ever receive benefits from a disability or critical illness policy, it is unlikely that you will characterize that period of your life as extraordinary. But it may turn out that your decision to arrange for these benefits was extraordinarily good planning. Understanding the risks is step one. Deciding what truly concerns you is step two. Finding the right protection and the right price is step three. Then when all is done the only thing left to do is forget about this issue and go on living a simply **extraordinary** life.

SIMPLE MONEY

Answer the following questions: If you were disabled, how much would you receive each month from current disability benefits? How do you qualify? For how long would benefits be paid? Will benefits rise over time to counter inflation? What isn't covered?

Don't like the answers to any of the above questions? Get help from a qualified advisor, and plug the gaps.

Understand the risks you face. Determine your level of concern with each risk. Find the right protection.

EXTRAORDINARY LIFE

A disability or a critical illness is not part of your plans for an extraordinary life. But, coverage for these may turn out to be extraordinarily good planning.

Once proper protection is in place, forget about this issue, and get on with your extraordinary life.

Chapter 8

Tax planning

It may seem like an oxymoron to say that taxes can be simple, but they can. You have other things to do and much more important things to worry about.

A brief historical perspective

It should come as no surprise that the history of taxes is filled with struggle and conflict. Evidence of tax collectors dates as far back as ancient Egypt where taxes were imposed on many items of daily living, including the cooking oil used in preparing the family meal. The Egyptians also imposed taxes on foreigners and slaves.

Raising funds for rulers in most civilizations throughout history has followed a two pronged approach: tax the citizens, conquer and steal from the enemies.

In 1404, England's parliament brought forth the first tax legislation. Not only was this ultimately defeated, but it was so vehemently opposed that all records were burned. In 1789, during the French Revolution, all tax collectors were found guilty of treason and sentenced to death by guillotine. Perhaps the most famous and least violent protest against taxes took place in 11th century England when Lady Godiva rode naked on a white horse in an effort to reduce the heavy tax burden imposed on the people by her husband, the Earl of Mercia.

War is the mother of taxes as we know them.

Tax legislation took hold in England in 1789 with the introduction of an income tax designed to fund the war against France. In the U.S., taxes were first signed into legislation by President Lincoln to fund the Civil War in 1861. Canada introduced income taxes in 1917 to fund the war efforts of World War I.

Conflict continues to be a central theme of taxes today. Many see taxes as a battleground, and the filing of one's income taxes each spring is one skirmish in the ongoing war between the government and the people. If that's the case, most would argue that the government has all the ammunition.

According to the Fraser Institute, (a highly respected independent public policy organization), the total tax bill for a Canadian family has risen 1,550% since 1961. They also estimate that currently, approximately 50% of the average household's income goes to some form of tax.

And so Canadians go to battle with the Canada Revenue Agency (formerly Revenue Canada), looking for any and every opportunity to reduce the tax burden. And like most great conflicts, often the real cause is lost in the heat of each emotional battle. We often lose sight of the things we **sacrifice** when struggling to save a few pennies in taxes.

The Simple Lesson

Most people believe that if they just understood more about the Tax Act, or were willing to invest in tax shelters, or had more money to work with, or were willing to take a more aggressive tax posture, they could dramatically reduce their income taxes. Nothing is quite as disappointing for most as the realization that none of these are true.

It's **impossible** to deny that the Tax Act is complicated, understood only by a few, and open to interpretation and exploitation. But one of the reasons for an increasingly complex tax system is the fact that when "loopholes" are discovered new legislation ultimately follows to close them down.

It may seem like giving up to simply take the attitude that one should pay taxes willingly, but when the opposite posture is taken it often leads to bitter legal battles and an unhealthy focus on the wrong aspects of life.

That's not to say one should be careless. It is the right of everyone to organize their affairs so as to minimize the tax owed. But for most people, this can be done quite simply. After that, it's best to get on with the other goals and issues at hand - issues that no doubt will lead to more extraordinary life experiences.

Putting the lesson to work

The Canadian income tax system is a progressive tax - meaning that taxes increase proportionately as income increases. Sales tax on the other hand is called regressive - it is a fixed percentage applied to each purchase regardless of the price, thus causing those with lower income to pay more as a percentage of their income. Income tax is considered by most to be fairer since the burden of tax decreases with income.

The rich pay **more** than the poor, because they can afford to do so.

There are two levels of income tax in Canada. The federal tax applies to all Canadians, and is supplemented in every province by the provincial tax. We rarely distinguish between the two taxes instead referring to our income tax as "combined." Two tax rates are commonly used in planning. The marginal tax rate is the rate used to calculate tax payable on the last dollar of income earned, while the average tax rate is simply the amount of tax paid divided by the total income earned.

In B.C., for example, an individual with an income of $50,000 would pay a total of $10,501 in combined federal and provincial tax. This represents an average tax rate of 21% (10,501/50,000). The marginal tax at $50,000, however, is 31.15%. So if this individual earns another $1 he would pay an additional 31 cents in income tax. The marginal tax rate in B.C, like most provinces, is banded into 8 different "tax brackets" with the highest marginal tax level hitting 43.70% on all income in excess of $115,739.

GOOD DEBT VS. BAD DEBT

You have heard about good debt and bad debt, and moreover that good debt can reduce your tax bill and increase your wealth. Should you be looking for good debt? Ultimately you are probably looking for no debt. Check out Chapter 10 for the full discussion.

Many people mistakenly believe that when they jump into a new income tax brack et it somehow affects the tax already paid at the lower levels. This is not true, and there is **no truth** to the rumour that a raise in pay can actually lower your take home pay due to an increase in taxes.

The issue of reducing taxes ultimately comes down to deductions and credits. deduction is just that, an item that you deduct from your total income before taxe are calculated. Deductions include child care expenses, RRSP contributions, an moving expenses. Since deductions reduce your taxable income, they are wort more if you are in a higher tax bracket. If you know your income is going to increas sharply in future years, it is sometimes wise to postpone claiming your deduction (if they can be carried forward) to capture the benefit of the higher tax rate.

Credits are amounts credited to you as if you had already paid that amount in taxe: They include the spousal credit, charitable donations, tuition fees, and medic: expenses. Credits are worth the same regardless of your tax bracket and should there fore be used as **soon as possible.**

Here are the various deductions and credits that you should be familiar with.

RRSP contributions

This is the biggie (it gets a chapter of its own). Every dollar deposited into an RRS during the calendar year or in the first 60 days of the following year can be deduct ed from your income before taxes are calculated. You may hear arguments agains the use of the RRSP, citing a better way, or perhaps a concern over paying even mor taxes when RRSP assets are ultimately withdrawn. There are cases in which th RRSP is not the best course of action, but these are rare. For most Canadians, th RRSP is by far the best way to simultaneously reduce taxes and save for retiremen and you should be making every effort to make maximum contributions every yea

Child care expenses

The cost of caring for children under the age of 17 is deductible, if those costs wer incurred to enable the parent to work or take occupational training. In all province except Quebec, the deduction must be made by the parent with the lowest income (thus minimizing the value of the deduction), and the total deduction cannot exceed two-thirds of that parent's income. For children up to age 7, the maximum deduction is $7,000 per child and for children between 7 and 16 the maximum is $4,000.

Moving Expenses

If you move to begin a new job (or start a business) and your new home is at least 40 km closer to your new job, then you can deduct most of the costs associated with the move. Included in those costs are: traveling costs, the cost of movers and rental equipment, the cost of selling your home, and legal bills on the purchase of the new home. The expenses can only be deducted against income earned at the new job or business, but can be carried forward to future years if you don't generate a profit as quickly as you had hoped.

LABOUR SPONSORED FUNDS

Despite recent plans by Government to eliminate, or curtail, the tax advantages of LSIFs, they continue to interest many, at least for now. Labour Sponsored Investment Funds (LSIF) generally make an appearance during the RRSP season and because of the tax credits available to investors they capture the attention of those planning to make a last minute contribution.

An RRSP contribution made by someone in the highest marginal tax level will generate a deduction that will save more than 40% in taxes. The combined tax credit on LSIFs in most provinces is at least 30%, making the tax savings for investing in an LSIF in your RRSP 70% or more! This is a very attractive arrangement, in fact, the 30% in tax credits could be considered the same as a 4.5% per annum lift in return over the 8 years that an LSIF is required to be held (if cashed sooner, penalties would apply and tax credits would have to be repaid.) Should you use them?

Cautiously, yes. Treat them as high risk, which they are. Don't let LSIFs comprise more than 5 to 10% of your RRSP or investment portfolio. And while the 4.5% head start may make them appear like winners out of the gate, keep in mind that in the past 5 years not one LSIF has shown a positive return. That means if you had earned 4.5% or more elsewhere you would have been better off.

Medical expenses

Medical expenses create a tax credit, but only on the amount that exceeds 3% of your net income. To maximize this credit, the spouse with the lowest income should claim the medical expenses for the entire family.

Education credit

Tuition fees and related expenses create a tax credit for students attending universities, colleges, and other post-secondary institutions. The cost of room and board is not given this status, but if the student is attending school full-time there is a monthly educational credit provided. If the student is unable to take advantage of the full amount of the available credit, a portion is transferable to a parent or grandparent.

Charitable donations

Gifts in cash or "in kind" (meaning you actually donate an item, such as a painting) made to a recognized charitable organization in Canada earn you a tax credit. The first $200 donated receives a tax credit that is calculated at the lowest marginal tax level, while gifts above that amount earn a credit equal to a deduction made at the highest marginal level.

Charitable donations can be claimed by either spouse and can be carried forward for up to five years. It's usually a good idea to have only one spouse claim all of the donations, and further to accumulate the receipts for up to five years to maximize the portion of those donations that fall above the $200 threshold.

Pension income credit

If you are receiving income from a life annuity, the first $1,000 per annum generates a tax credit. The Old Age Security and Canada Pension Plan do not qualify for this deduction. Annuities from an RRSP or RRIF may qualify, but only if you are 65 or older, or receiving benefits due to the death of a spouse.

As well as this list of deductions and credits (and others that may not be listed here) there are also a few tips and strategies that you should incorporate into your overall financial plan.

IS YOUR TAX TAIL WAGGING THE DOG?

Don't let the tax tail wag the dog. Ever wonder exactly what that means? A number of investors have found out over the years, and to put things into perspective let's consider one specific example.

Vern bought a number of shares in Bell Canada in 1985 to add to his modest portfolio. He believed in buying stock for the long haul, and hung on to those shares, allowing the dividend reinvestment program to increase the number of shares gradually over the years. By 1999 those shares had grown nicely, but not nearly as well as the shares of the company Bell had spun off a few years prior – Nortel Networks.

Near the peak of the market, Vern's holdings in Nortel exceeded $600,000. In reviewing his overall financial position I pointed out that his holdings in this one security now represented more than 50% of his total net worth. While pointing out that I was not able to advise him with respect to the specific security (not being a qualified stock broker), I was nonetheless able to tell him that uncategorically, when any single investment other than your home reaches that proportion of your total net worth your investments are out of balance.

Vern agreed, and he even suggested that he was uncomfortable holding this particular company – he didn't know much about it but was pretty sure that no company was as good as all this. Still, if he sold out now, his tax bill would be in excess of $120,000. I suggested he consider selling some, or establishing a program to reduce his holdings gradually over time. In the end, he did nothing, and as the market came crashing down his investment shrunk to a few thousand dollars. This is a case of the tax tail wagging the dog.

For many who held similar investments a tax decision led to a disaster. Always make investment decisions based on the investment first, and the tax consequences second.

File each year, and file on time

For the 2002 tax year, more than 1.7 million Canadians filed late, adding $36.4 million dollars to Government coffers in late fees and penalties. If taxes are war, this is one battle that individuals are clearly losing.

Late filing has other costs, including the emotional effects caused by uncertainty not to mention breaking a law. It is also possible that late filing may cause a chain in which other opportunities are **missed,** like contributing to an RRSP.

MEET MARK MITCHELL

Mark Mitchell came into my office one day a few years ago with a bone to pick. He had been speaking to several of his buddies at the office and they had all just received a large refund on their tax return thanks to a tax shelter that was known as the "buy-low-donate-high scheme." He was quite upset that I hadn't recommended such an arrangement, or at least made him aware that this was available.

"Well Mike," I responded "I won't pretend that I ever plan to tell you about every 'scheme' that exists for shaving tax dollars." I put a little emphasis on the word 'scheme' to make sure he realized he had chosen that word. "First of all, I won't possibly know about them all. And more importantly, I don't recommend them."

"Why not?" he asked with a look of disbelief.

"Tell me what you know about this particular shelter," I asked politely.

"Well, I know that George put $10,000 into this thing and got over $14,000 back on his tax return. What else do I need to know?"

"In my opinion plenty, but maybe that's just me." I countered. "Let me tell you what I know."

I proceeded to explain that this particular scheme probably involved medical supplies, which were purchased using the $10,000 that George had invested, and then donated to a hospital or medical facility. The hospital or medical facility in turn would provide the donor with a charitable receipt, and based on George's tax refund that receipt would show a donation of at least $35,000. In effect then George bought low and donated for a higher receipt, an amount so high that the tax refund exceeded his actual purchase price providing a nice quick return.

Use a Spousal RRSP

A spousal RRSP has absolutely no tax advantage today over a regular RRSP. The contributing spouse gets the tax relief, just has he or she would have if that contribution had been made to a personal RRSP. But since the funds now reside in the spouse's plan, when those funds are eventually withdrawn the income and hence the tax on that income will have been shifted from the contributor to the spouse.

Mike was calming down, but still agitated. "Okay," he said, "It sounds a little shady. But, it worked. They have their refunds! Why do I always miss these things?"

"Just because they appear to be an approved tax shelter, and even though your friends have their tax refunds, that doesn't mean CRA is going to leave it alone. There are a number of stated positions on this type of tax scheme coming from CRA and they all say the same thing: the CRA doesn't like them. They will continue to investigate and you and I both know they can audit your returns for up to seven years, at least. And if these shelters end up being disallowed, your friends may be facing repayment of the tax savings plus penalties and interest. If you want in on that kind of action, you should ask your friends for the name of their advisor."

Mike was silent for a moment. Then he sighed as he said, "I wonder if it really pays to always do the right thing."

"I'm not sure it's about some universal right or wrong Mike," I offered. "I think it's simply a matter of doing what's right for you. Before you can do that, you need the facts. Based on what you know now, what would you like to do?"

Mike laughed as he got up to leave and ended our discussion with, "I think I'd like to have fewer facts."

Not too long after our meeting a story in the press suggested that many of the buy-low-donate-high schemes were under investigation and it was anticipated that many of the donors would be facing a repayment of tax refunds. Remembering Mike's request to have less not more information I resisted the temptation to send him a copy of the story. But I did stick it in his file, just in case he brings it up in the future.

Use RESPs or in-trust accounts to shift income to children

Both of these plans provide a lift in your efforts to save for your children's future, by effectively shifting some or all of the future income generated by investments into the hands of your children. The real reason to use these tools of course is to help your children – the tax advantages simply magnify your efforts.

Start a business

There are many tax advantages provided to the self-employed that make it an attractive option, (although this alone is not reason enough to leave a job and venture into
business). For example, you may be able to claim certain expenses incurred for operating your business at home, you may hire a spouse or child and thus split income
and you may be able to deduct a portion of expenses incurred for travel and enter-
tainment. Keep in mind, this is not intended to be a perk for "going it alone."
Expenses are only allowed when they are reasonable and documented.

Arrange your investments in a tax-smart manner

Not all income is taxed equally. As discussed in Chapter 5, capital gains
and dividends receive preferential treatment. To the extent that they fit into your
overall risk/return profile, they should be included in your investment portfolio as
much to generate the potential higher returns as to reduce taxes. However, inside an
RRSP, investments are not subject to tax, so tax treatment doesn't matter. If you have
investments both inside and outside an RRSP you should consider all of your investments as one portfolio and allocate the tax efficient investments to your non-registered account and the interest bearing investments to your RRSP. This way, you
preserve the overall asset allocation of your investments while reducing your taxes.

ALTERNATIVE MINIMUM TAX

In the ongoing battle to eliminate tax loopholes and keep the rich from ducking their fair share of income
tax, the Alternative Minimum Tax (AMT) was introduced in 1986. This system is actually a separate way
of calculating tax that eliminates some of the deductions and credits on large incomes. Intended to flush
out individuals who are going overboard with tax shelters and aggressive planning strategies, unfortunately it may also affect those who for whatever reason just happened to receive an unusually large sum
of money. For example, someone who has received a severance and attempts to put a large amount into
their RRSP to catch up on unused contributions may find that the AMT blocks part of that strategy.
If you think the AMT may apply call an accountant and get some help.

Use cash value life insurance

A review of the chapter on life insurance will reveal that permanent insurance can be structured to include a savings account that is not subject to taxation. If you have already earmarked a chunk of wealth to be passed on to the next generation, this strategy is most likely your best means of doing it. If you aren't so sure, then you need to tread carefully to make sure that the cost of insurance and potential penalties for early withdrawal won't ultimately make this a losing proposition. Still, apart from the RRSP, this is the only real tax shelter available to us, so it's worth a look.

Get help

If you are not sure that you are fully utilizing the tax planning advantages available to you, or you are starting to get confused with the various forms and schedules, the simplest and probably smartest thing to do is get help. Yes, accountants charge a fee, but in the end most of them will save you money. And all of them will save you **time** and reduce your **anxiety,** letting you get on with more important matters.

Summary

A great number of things regarding money can cause us needless stress, and certainly taxes are among them. No-one wants to pay too much, but in the end none of us would object to paying our fair share. Our infrastructure and social system depends on our tax dollars. But income tax is one of those things in which it often appears that the other guy is getting something you aren't. The resulting frustration (that really has no solution since that "something" can never be found) leads us far off the path of the extraordinary life.

SIMPLE MONEY	EXTRAORDINARY LIFE
Hire an accountant.	There are countless things in life more important than taxes. Worry about them. Better yet, enjoy them.

Chapter 9

RRSPs

If this is **all** you do financially, an extraordinary life is almost assured.

A brief historical perspective

The Registered Retirement Savings Plan was passed into legislation in 1957, almost ten years prior to the creation of the public pension plan (CPP) and more than two decades ahead of similar legislation south of the border. The current generation of Canadians then should be entrenched in the belief that planning for retirement is largely a personal matter. That doesn't seem to be the case.

Next to the personal residence, the RRSP is the single biggest asset for Canadians. However, the average RRSP balance is currently around $42,000. Given that the average age of RRSP holders is mid-forties, most experts suggest that we are likely to find ourselves in a heap of trouble as retirement age approaches.

The numbers certainly don't look good. The average annual contribution to an RRSP is approximately $5,000, but more than 1,000,000 Canadians took money out of their RRSPs last year (excluding those who withdrew to purchase a home). Just over half of those eligible to contribute to an RRSP made a contribution last year. Perhaps most alarming is our declining use of the RRSP. In 1991 Canadians only used 27% of the maximum available RRSP contribution room. By 1996 that had dropped to 12%, and by 2004 it was approaching 10%. In other words 90% of the available room is being left unused – and the best opportunity for Canadians to retire comfortably is largely being **ignored.**

The simple lesson

An RRSP allows us to enjoy a number of valuable benefits. Contributions to an RRSP reduce your taxable income, and subsequently, the amount of tax you pay. Growth within the RRSP from dividends, interest or capital gains is not taxable each year, but rather deferred until funds are eventually withdrawn. While the funds are intended for retirement, they remain accessible in case of an important financial need. And if income in retirement is lower than income during working years, it is possible to not only defer but actually reduce your overall tax bill.

With very few exceptions, this is as good as it's going to get for any type of investment plan. We should be using it to the fullest extent possible. Furthermore, if started young enough, the RRSP, combined with existing government benefits such as CPP and OAS, should more than satisfy the retirement income needs for most of us.

Here then is the simple lesson: make maximum contributions to your RRSP each year. Invest the funds in your RRSP based on the lessons in Chapter 5. If you are behind in your RRSP contributions, plan to get caught up as soon as possible.

If this is *all* you do financially, an extraordinary life is **almost assured.**

HOW YOUR RRSP FITS INTO THE BIG PICTURE

Since RRSP assets are not subject to tax while assets outside an RRSP usually are, it makes sense to look at your overall portfolio and manage both to minimize the overall tax bill. If, for example, you have a mixture of fixed income and equities in both your RRSP and non-registered accounts, you have a well balanced portfolio, but you may be paying more tax than you need to. As much as possible, move the equities to your non-registered account, and your fixed income to your RRSP account. You can maintain the same overall weightings, and thus not change either the expected volatility or return of your overall investments. At the same time, you will reduce your tax bill, which in turn will speed up your accumulation of wealth.

Putting the lesson to work

RRSP basics

- Each year you are allowed to contribute 18% of the prior year's income to your RRSP, up to an overall maximum (which in 2007 is $19,000).
- The limit is reduced by any amount contributed to a company pension plan last year, either by you or your employer.
- If you don't make the maximum contribution you can "carry forward" the unused amount indefinitely.
- Every dollar contributed to an RRSP reduces your taxable income for the year by one dollar.
- You can contribute to an RRSP up until the year in which you turn 71, at which time your RRSP must be converted to either an annuity or a RRIF (Registered Retirement Income Fund).
- When money is extracted from an RRSP, either prior to or during retirement (including from a RRIF or annuity that started as an RRSP), every dollar is included in your income and taxed accordingly.
- A wide range of investments can be held inside an RRSP, including GICs, individual securities and mutual funds.

Self-directed RRSPs

You can open an RRSP with a specific institution, (such as a bank or mutual fund company), and hold only specific investments offered by the holding institution. This is common with GICs for example. The other option is a self-directed RRSP. These enable you to hold a variety of investments even from a variety of different institutions within the same RRSP account. A self-directed RRSP will often carry a fee payable to the holding institution known as a trustee fee, usually in the range of $50 to $175 per year.

The self-directed plan is by far the most popular - and for good reason. Since most long term investment accounts hold more than one asset type and since your diversification strategy might include investments managed by different companies, the self-directed plan allows you to do this without the hassle of having multiple accounts.

RRSP vs. non-registered

Fairly regularly, someone in the financial press will attack the RRSP and suggest that there are far better alternatives. One of those alternatives will be paying down debt, which for most is not superior (see Chapter 10 - Debt for a complete analysis). The other alternative is save for retirement in a non-registered account. Let's look at that option.

Let's suppose that you earn $50,000 per year, and can therefore contribute $9,000 per year to your RRSP (18% of $50,000). That's $750 per month. If you did this faithfully for 25 years, and your RRSP earned 8% per annum, you would end up with $713,269 in your RRSP.

Each year your $9,000 contribution would generate a tax refund. Assuming a marginal tax rate of 31%, (the approximate rate in Ontario on $50,000 of income), that refund would equal $2,790. That means you really only need to come up with $6,210 of your own money ($9,000 – 6,210), or $517.50 per month after accounting for the tax refund.

Let's take that same out-of-pocket cost and invest it in a non-registered account. $517.50 per month for 25 years at the same rate of return (8%) would result in a value of $481,871. Obviously this doesn't look better, but the argument hinges on the taxes paid on the money as it is being spent, or in a worst case scenario, when it is left behind to children.

Withdrawals from an RRSP or RRIF are considered regular income, whereas the non-registered account could be set up to pay taxes at the much lower level afforded capital gains. If you could somehow manage to create a non-registered portfolio without triggering or paying any capital gains, interest, or dividends for 25 years, you would have achieved the ultimate in tax minimization. Let's use that as an ideal scenario. Tax then would be payable on the deferred gain – essentially the difference between what you put in and what you get out – at half the normal rate. (Capital gains currently enjoy a 50% inclusion rate).

Look at the table below to see the after tax values of our two scenarios.

TO RRSP OR NOT TO RRSP - SCENARIO ONE

	RRSP	NON-REGISTERED
Value 25yrs	$713,269	$481,871
ACB (how much you put in)	N/A	$155,250
Taxable gain	N/A	$326,621
Tax rate	46.41%	23.2%
Tax payable	$331,028	$75,776
Net value	$382,240	$406,094

But I have assumed in this scenario that the tax rate on withdrawal is at today's highest marginal rates (for Ontario). What if the tax rate was the same at both the time of deposit and the time of withdrawal? To illustrate, let's assume that you are in the highest marginal tax rate today and in retirement (in both cases 46.41%). The RRSP refund is going to be higher each year, leading to a lower "out of pocket" expense and therefore a lower contribution to non-registered savings in order to keep our assumptions on equal footing.

TO RRSP OR NOT TO RRSP - SCENARIO TWO

	RRSP	NON-REGISTERED
Value 25yrs	$713,269	$374,258
ACB (how much you put in)	N/A	$120,579
Taxable gain	N/A	$253,679
Tax rate	46.41%	23.2%
Tax payable	$331,028	$58,853
Net value	$382,240	$315,405

In this case the RRSP comes out a **clear winner.**

So, yes, an argument can be made for a better strategy than the RRSP. But it hinges on creating a non-registered account that generates little to no tax, and this can lead to making poor financial decisions based on taxation instead of sound investment principles. Furthermore, it assumes that taxes payable on withdrawal will exceed the taxes saved when depositing. If you expect to withdraw funds at a similar tax rate to your marginal rate now **the RRSP is clearly a superior option.**

Yes, if your RRSP passes to someone other than a spouse, on death it would be taxed at the highest marginal rate, despite the fact that you may be in a lower tax bracket today. But, planning to have less in retirement so that you can leave more behind always strikes me as a particularly poor planning strategy.

In almost all cases, the RRSP is the most sensible, simplest, and most productive means of accumulating funds for a long and happy retirement. Use it to its fullest.

RRSPs and government benefits

Another argument against the RRSP contends that because RRSP income is taxed higher than capital gains, or even dividends, the income stream created by an RRSP, especially after age 69 when funds must be withdrawn, may cause government benefits – specifically OAS – to be clawed back.

In a few cases this will be true. But whether or not a clawback will occur is extremely difficult to predict until retirement is imminent, making it a dubious argument for those who should be pouring money into an RRSP. The fact is, if you are building a retirement plan around securing the maximum income available from government benefits, you may be missing the point of financial planning. Independence is valuable; certainly in this case worth the few dollars that may be sacrificed in order to have the funds yourself to live the life you want, without having to rely on the government.

This kind of planning should be entertained only by those few people who might depend on government benefits to survive, or are very close to retirement and are considering further contributions to an RRSP account.

Making regular contributions

Contributions made to your RRSP in the calendar year, plus during the first 60 days of the following year, can be deducted from your income for that taxation year. The "deadline" then for RRSP contributions generally falls on March 1, and consequently the month of February is generally considered "RRSP season."

In this case a deadline is both a good thing and a bad thing. It's good in that it pushes people into action, encouraging them to make a last minute contribution to an RRSP in order to generate a tax refund a few months later. It's bad in that it causes a large number of people to believe that this is actually when they should be making those contributions.

The best time to contribute is **as soon as you possibly can.** January 1st each year would be a good time to make your maximum RRSP contribution for the year. For most people this is not possible for a variety of reasons. The best strategy for most is a monthly contribution all year, adjusted each April or May to ensure that the amount deposited by the end of February of the next year is equal to the maximum allowed. This is the best way for two reasons. First, it's easier to make small monthly contributions than it is to come up with a lump sum at the deadline. Second, it puts your RRSP on "autopilot," creating a positive financial habit and taking advantage of dollar cost averaging.

THE END OF FOREIGN CONTENT

Legislation that recently passed has finally ended the ongoing debate about foreign content inside and RRSP and eliminated the need for various sophisticated (and more expensive) strategies that had been designed to circumvent the former rules. But the question remains – how much foreign content should I have in my RRSP? The answer to that lies in understanding your overall asset allocation strategy (see Chapter 5). Just because the limit used to be 30% doesn't mean you should have at least that much. For many people, 30% remains a good target. For others, it may be more or less. It's best to forget about these old rules and focus instead on what is going to work best for you.

Dollar cost averaging

You may hear some financial commentators speak about dollar cost averaging (DCA) as if it were magic, while others will put it down as misleading and damaging. The fact is, it's merely a simple way of investing that reduces the stress of worrying about the "right time" to invest. And during market downturns, this strategy can actually help to smooth out or even increase returns.

Consider two investors. Mr. Bull believes the market is going to go up and plunks down $6,000 in the ABC Investment Fund, currently trading at $10 per unit. Mr. Bear decides to invest monthly and over the next 12 months he puts $500 each month into the same fund. At the end of the year both have invested a total $6,000. Now let's consider two different scenarios. (See table)

THE POWER OF DOLLAR COST AVERAGING – SCENARIO 1: MARKET GOES DOWN

MONTH	UNIT VALUE	UNITS OWNED	MR. BULL'S BALANCE	UNITS OWNED	MR. BEAR'S BALANCE
1	$10.00	600	$6,000	50	$500
2	$9.50	600	$5,700	102.6	$975
3	$8.75	600	$5,250	159.8	$1,398
4	$7.00	600	$4,200	231.2	$1,618
5	$6.00	600	$3,600	314.5	$1,887
6	$6.00	600	$3,600	397.9	$2,387
7	$5.00	600	$3,000	497.9	$2,489
8	$4.50	600	$2,700	609.0	$2,740
9	$6.00	600	$3,600	692.3	$4,154
10	$6.75	600	$4,050	766.4	$5,173
11	$8.00	600	$4,800	828.9	$6,631
12	$10.00	600	$6,000	878.9	$8,789

In scenario 1, the market goes down, then rebounds so that at the end of the year the unit values are where they started. In this scenario Mr. Bull has $6,000 at the end of the year, but Mr. Bear has $8,789! Mr. Bull invested the entire $6,000 at $10 per unit. Since that's where the investment fund ended he neither gained nor

RRSPs

lost any money. Mr. Bear on the other hand invested $500 at $10 per unit, but he also invested $500 each month at much lower unit values – including month 8 in which unit values had dropped to $4.50. So when the unit values rose to their previous level of $10 Mr. Bear had seen **substantial growth** on parts of his overall investment.

THE POWER OF DOLLAR COST AVERAGING - SCENARIO 2: MARKET GOES UP

MONTH	UNIT VALUE	UNITS OWNED	MR. BULL'S BALANCE	UNITS OWNED	MR. BEAR'S BALANCE
1	$10.00	600	$6,000	50	$500
2	$10.10	600	$6,060	99.5	$1,005
3	$10.12	600	$6,072	148.9	$1,507
4	$10.18	600	$6,108	198.0	$2,016
5	$10.20	600	$6,120	247.0	$2,520
6	$10.22	600	$6,132	296.0	$3,025
7	$10.23	600	$6,138	344.8	$3,528
8	$10.30	600	$6,180	393.4	$4,052
9	$10.25	600	$6,150	442.2	$4,532
10	$10.35	600	$6,210	490.5	$5,076
11	$10.40	600	$6,240	538.6	$5,601
12	$10.50	600	$6,300	586.2	$6,155

In scenario 2, we assume that the market simply increases gradually, realizing an overall return of 5% by year end. In this case, Mr. Bull comes out ahead, since each month Mr. Bear invests his $500 at increasing prices, thus buying fewer and fewer units each time. If we make the increase in prices more dramatic of course Mr. Bear would fall **farther and farther behind.**

So the argument against dollar cost averaging is that in rising markets it reduces your return, which is true. The argument for dollar cost averaging is that in falling markets it will increase your long term returns. Keep in mind, however, that you generally can't expect the recovery to occur within one year as illustrated.

For many, investing monthly is simply the **easiest way to do it,** and so dollar cost averaging occurs by default. But even for those with the capital to invest all at once, if you are concerned about the possibility of a falling market spreading your investment out over the year can reduce this risk as well as your stress.

The key thing is to determine a strategy that is best for you and stick with it.

Borrowing to top up your RRSP

Should you borrow to top up your RRSP? Take a look at Chapter 10 for a discussion on debt vs. RRSP, because that is really what this boils down to. In brief the answer is yes if you believe that the returns inside the RRSP will outpace the cost of the loan (and keep in mind that the loan is not tax deductible). The answer is no if you are concerned that this may not work out that way, or if getting out of debt is a higher priority.

If you don't borrow to catch up on unused contribution room, you should at least attempt to contribute enough each year so that the unused room is shrinking. Perhaps take out a small loan if necessary to make this happen. While debt can be a real psychological burden (and in most cases should be avoided) RRSPcontribution room that is soaring beyond reasonable levels can be just as much of a burden. Eventually, you start to wonder if you will ever "catch up." This can lead to a feeling that you are way off track with respect to retirement planning. You don't have to be making big gains, but by at least moving in the right direction you can often increase the sense of financial well-being, and that's important for a simple and extraordinary life.

Spousal RRSP

The spousal RRSP provides a wonderful opportunity to split income and thus reduce taxes by leveling the income received by each spouse in retirement.

To determine whether a spousal RRSP is appropriate, you need to determine whether there's likely to be a considerable imbalance in retirement income. If for example Mrs. Smith has remained home to raise a family while the Mr. Smith has worked, chances are Mr. Smith will have accumulated retirement assets and perhaps be part of a pension plan at work, while Mrs. Smith has nothing to look forward to but the potential of government benefits.

MEET JEAN AND RICK TANDY

Like many Canadians, Jean and Rick Tandy felt as though their savings program was in slow motion. They each contributed $100 per month to a personal RRSP. Jean was also saving $100 per pay period ($200 a month) into a Canada Savings Bond via payroll deduction. Rick was also participating in a payroll deduction savings plan at work at a rate of $150 per month. Finally, they were putting $200 per month into a joint-non-registered account that had no particular purpose attached to it, but would probably be used for a home renovation or vacation. They had no children yet, but planned to one day, and they wondered how they would be able to meet those expenses with an already stretched budget.

A financial plan showed the Tandys that things weren't all that bad. The fact that they were saving $750 per month had already allowed them to accumulate more than $40,000 in savings in the various accounts. But they could do much more with no more effort if we focused on the RRSP instead of the other savings accounts.

Jean was rising quickly up the corporate ladder and had just received a raise taking her income to $78,000 per year. Rick was a self-employed consultant and had been consistently earning in the range of $45,000 each year for several years. This made contributions to Jean's RRSP a much more attractive option – her marginal tax rate was now over 43%, while Rick's was only 31%. Both Jean and Rick had more than $20,000 of RRSP contribution available, so I recommended that they contribute only to Jean's RRSP at least until her RRSP room was exhausted or circumstances changed.

Based on the current numbers, only $200 of the Tandys $750 in savings was generating a tax refund. The contribution of $1,200 for the year was generating a refund of $520.92 for Jean and $373.80 for Rick for a total of $894.72. If we put the entire $750 each month to Jean's RRSP, the refund would be $3,906.90 – an increase of $3,012.18!

The Tandy's initial reaction was resistance. They didn't want to "lock-in" the money inside the RRSP, especially only in Jean's name. But we discussed using a spousal RRSP for a portion of the contribution to keep their personal accounts in balance, and when I pointed out that a good portion of their current savings was already outside the RRSP and would remain available for unexpected expenses, they began to see the overwhelming benefits. In fact, Jean eventually said, "What if we take our current non-registered savings and move them into our RRSP accounts to get caught up?"

"Now you are catching on," I said. And in fact a portion of their non-registered savings *did* find its way into the RRSP, and the additional tax savings was used to replenish those funds. Suddenly both of them felt as though things were moving along a whole lot faster.

This being the case, Mr. Smith can make contributions to a spousal RRSP. Mr. Smith still receives the tax deduction and can only make contributions as per his personal RRSP contribution limit. But, the assets now belong to Mrs. Smith and in retirement, she will make the withdrawals and be taxed on the income.

The objective is to balance retirement incomes as much as possible, or at least have both spouses in the same marginal tax bracket (if both spouses will be in the highest tax bracket anyway, the spousal RRSP strategy would have little purpose).

Taking money out of the RRSP before retirement

Don't. There are probably other options, such as borrowing, that will be much less damaging to your net worth.

There may be exceptions of course, such as the home buyer's plan or the life long learning plan. Both of these plans allow you to "borrow" from your own RRSP by withdrawing funds without paying tax, so long as you replace the borrowed funds within specified time frames. The rule here is to use them only as a **last resort,** and repay them as soon as possible.

Taking money out of the RRSP at retirement

Until you are 69 you can simply take money out of your RRSP "as needed." However, this is rarely a good idea. Some planning should be done of course, but generally funds in a non-registered investment should be used first since the tax bill will be lower.

Once you turn 69, you must convert all RRSP accounts to RRIF accounts and begin making withdrawals the following year based on minimum levels set by CRA. There is no need to change your investments when converting from an RRSP to a RRIF, but you should ensure that sufficient "short term" investments are in place to cover the withdrawals to be made.

An annuity is another option available at any time. An annuity provides a guaranteed income stream for a specified period of time – usually for the lifetime of the investor, known as the annuitant. It is common to name a spouse as a joint annuitant so that the income stream, or a portion of it at least, would continue to that spouse should they live longer. For many retirees, the idea of a guaranteed income is attractive, and in some cases, this is the best option. However, an annuity should only be considered if the guarantee of regular income for life is the highest priority. The downside of the annuity is that in most cases, no benefits are passed down to children or other heirs.

The final word on RRSPs is this:

use them to the full extent that you can. When used as intended, they will often single handedly fill the gap between what you need and what you will already get in government and employee pensions. Left unused, they serve as a regular reminder of the fact that you are falling behind.

Open an RRSP, and invest monthly. This is the "pay yourself first" advice that is really the universal truth about getting rich in the simplest way possible. Your RRSP assets will grow and ultimately provide you with a continuation of the extraordinary life beyond your working years.

SIMPLE MONEY

Self-directed RRSP accounts allow for optimal diversification.

There isn't a better way to save for retirement.

Invest monthly – it forms a good habit, makes you feel good about taking action each month, and utilizes dollar cost averaging to help smooth out returns.

Borrow for your RRSP if you are comfortable with debt, and there is no other way.

Use a spousal income to split retirement income with a spouse.

Don't take money out of your RRSP before retirement.

EXTRAORDINARY LIFE

The RRSP along with government benefits is probably enough to ensure a long prosperous retirement!

Chapter 10

Debt

For most people, a debt-free existence is practically unimaginable. Start imagining. Start planning. It's easier than you think. It's better than you can imagine.

A brief historical perspective

For as long as there has been "money," there has been debt. Tablets from Mesopotamia dating back more than 3,000 years show how records were kept about who owed what to whom.

The earliest record of interest being charged on money belongs to the Sumerians. Their word for interest, "mash" is the same word used for calf. This idea of "giving birth" to money was also adopted by the Egyptians whose word for interest literally meant "to give birth."

The idea of new life, of multiplying one's wealth, is indeed an attractive one – for the lender charging interest. For those paying interest the history of debt is much more unpleasant. In fact, throughout history many societies and religious groups have stood in direct opposition to lending money. It was argued that charging interest was a form of "unearned" income and was therefore in direct conflict with the laws of nature or God's laws. Income was to be earned through work, effort, initiative and enterprise. Furthermore, charging interest exploited the needy and resulted in expanding the divide between the rich and the poor.

We might like to think that excessive debt is a modern phenomenon - a direct result of the easy access to credit in our electronic age. **Not so.** Excessive debt has been a problem throughout history and the cost of borrowing has always been more than the stated rate of interest. In the earliest instances of credit those unable to repay their debts could possibly lose their farms or livelihoods, be cast into slavery, or be forced to turn over loved ones.

Luckily, as financial systems became more sophisticated and regulated, more civilized penalties were instituted, from public humiliation in the pillory, to imprisonment. A stay in debtor's prison became an increasingly common occurrence, so much so in fact that England created the first real bankruptcy laws in 1570 to deal with over-crowded jail cells. The same statute gave the state the power to execute uncoopera-tive debtors, and a 1604 amendment permitted the debtor's ear to be cut off.

Samuel Johnson wrote in 1758:

> It is vain to continue an institution which experience shows to be ineffectual. We have now imprisoned one generation of debtors after another, but we do not find that their numbers lessen. We have now learned, that rashness and imprudence will not be deterred from taking credit; let us try whether fraud and avarice may be more easily restrained from giving it.

Dr. Johnson's suggestion has most certainly been tried, although most would argue without reaching a satisfactory conclusion. The availability of credit has expanded over the past two centuries. Anyone involved in selling a product has discovered that offering credit increases sales. As the automobiles rolled off the lines at Henry Ford's new plant in the early 1900s, their cost was almost half a year's income to the average worker. Ford wasn't yet in the finance business, so third-party companies emerged to help car buyers. By 1924 75% of the autos purchased were financed with installment loans.

The biggest change in the history of credit is perhaps the introduction of the credit card in 1950 by Diner's Club. The plastic credit card brought with it a host of con-veniences, but two notable changes. First, the merchant no longer would have to play lender and take on all the risks that came along with that role. And more impor-tantly from the consumer's viewpoint no longer would you need to stay away from the grocery store to avoid a confrontation with the grocer if you had an unpaid bill.

Today, credit is considered a **financial necessity** and young adults obtain some form of loan or credit card simply to establish a good credit rating. Owning a home is no longer simply a lifestyle decision, it's a key financial decision, as the ownership opens up a vast array of options to use the equity in the home as a loan to do something else - be that renovate, travel, or simply buy more stuff. As home prices have risen and interest rates fallen, our appetite for credit has soared. Over the past 10 years, the average Canadian's personal debt load has grown at **twice** the rate as personal income.

On average, every Canadian has at least two credit cards, a mortgage, a line of credit, and a car loan. Our debts already far exceed our annual income, and we carry in our wallets the power to add to that tens of thousands of dollars in additional debt without having to beg for permission. More ways to get into debt arrive in our mailbox daily. Credit is marketed more aggressively today than ever in history, and credit card companies are more than willing to sign you up even at the risk that you may not be able to repay.

The thing to learn from history is this: borrowing money has a price and only **part** of that price is **more money.**

The Simple Lesson

It is tempting to simply say don't borrow money, but as unfortunate as it may be, that is difficult advice in the society we live in. Owning a home and even an automobile would be next to impossible for most were it not for the ability to finance both. And while the cost of financing adds significantly to the ultimate cost of these major purchases, in the end we would all agree they are important and worthy of the additional expense.

So the simple lesson that we should learn is this: borrow as little as possible as cheaply as you can and repay it as quickly as you are able. Strive to be debt-free.

Putting the lesson to work

No doubt you have heard about good debt and bad debt, and if so, you may assume that my simple lesson refers to bad debt only. You would be wrong. In my opinion, there is no such thing as good debt. Obviously there are degrees of difference, but the label "good" is **too strong** and in some instances the label "bad" is **too weak.**

The best possible debt is that which enables you to accomplish something important, like own a home, get an education, or obtain medical assistance. In these cases, the debt isn't good, but rather acceptable or necessary. You certainly don't want to keep the debt, and you will make it a high priority to repay it as soon as you can.

Credit card debt on a retail card at 24% per annum isn't bad, it's disastrous, and if left unchecked it can lead to financial and emotional stress and even financial ruin.

Quite often the "good" vs. "bad" debate is really a reference to tax deductibility, with deductible debt winning the nod as good debt. Certainly tax deductible debt is generally better, but it's not because it's deductible, it's because the tax savings make it cheaper. Suppose you have two debts. One is charging you 4%, and it is not deductible. The other is charging you 6% and it is a tax deductible. Which should you pay off first? That will depend. If you are in a 40% tax bracket, the 6% interest cost becomes 3.6% (60% of 6%). You should pay off the non-deductible debt first. If however you are in a 30% tax bracket the 6% interest becomes 4.2% (70% of 6%). In that case you should pay off the deductible debt first. So, which is the "good" debt?

Once again, that depends.

So, can we make our debt deductible? The only provision in the tax act (based on the rules in place in late 2006) that allows for the deduction of interest payments is when the funds are being used to generate income. You can therefore borrow to operate a business. You can deduct a portion of your mortgage interest if you generate rental income by renting out a portion of your house. And, although this is currently the subject of much debate and scrutiny by government, you can deduct the interest on loans used for investment purposes.

Any of these things may receive the "good" label from many financial gurus. I still maintain that **no debt is by far best.**

Borrowing to invest

The advantages of borrowing to invest, or "leverage" are easy to see. Let's say you borrow $10,000 at a rate of 6%, and you invest that money at 7%. After one year you would owe $600 in interest. But since this is tax deductible, if you were in a 30% marginal tax bracket, your real interest costs would only be $420. You earned $700 and even if this was taxed at your marginal level you would still keep $490 for a net gain of $70. In other words you made $70 with none of your own money. It's almost magic. If you could somehow defer the tax on the earnings (which in theory you can), you would keep $280 ($700 - $420) of your earnings. Now borrow $100,000 and your net earnings grow to $2,800. We could keep going of course.

Leveraged investing, especially when using the tax deductibility of interest, is indeed a powerful tool. The fact is, leveraged investing can magnify your returns almost without limit – in our example earning any amount with no investment is actually incalculable, or infinite for the mathematically inclined. But if your investment goes down instead of up your losses can be just as **infinite.**

Leverage only works if you are able to take risks with your investments – in other words, you can't leverage and play it safe. If your cost of borrowing exceeds the net gain on your investment, you are losing ground.

THE NOT-SO-SIMPLE LIFE

The trend over the past decade has clearly been towards complexity. The average Canadian has 9 different banking products spread over 2 different financial institutions. We want "easy" access to our money, and we want to obtain credit with the least amount of effort. It's easier to establish a second line of credit at a new institution than it is to refinance the mortgage or ask an existing lender to raise the line of credit to a higher level. And so things get more complicated. This is certainly not a path towards anything extraordinary. Simplify! Consolidate! Stop taking the easy road and take the road towards your goals.

Let's take the same $10,000 borrowed at 6%. If after one year your return on the investment is 3%, your gain even before tax is only $300, an amount insufficient to cover the after tax cost of the loan, which is $420. Leveraged investing requires you to invest in such a way that your gain exceeds your costs – and this likely means equities. Equities go up and down. If you are prone to experiencing stress when your investment portfolio is losing value, particularly when you have borrowed those funds, then leverage is a very bad idea. And keep in mind: your investments at some point in the cycle are going to go down.

It would appear to me that leveraged investing is one of those catch-22 issues in the financial world. You should only do it if you can afford to take a substantial loss or have plenty of time to recover from those losses. If that's the case, I wonder why one might need to find ways to accelerate wealth accumulation.

The mortgage dilemma – short or long, fixed or variable?

When negotiating or renewing a mortgage, most people spend an inordinate amount of time fretting over interest rates. Are interest rates going up, which means we should lock into a long term mortgage, or are they going down, which means we should go short - or even variable?

Trying to predict the future of interest rates is next to impossible. So stop trying. The mortgage decision should be made on completely different criteria: your personality.

Some people are unable to sleep easy with any financial product that has a variable unpredictable rate. They crave certainty and want to be able to predict with the highest possible degree of accuracy their income and expenses well into the future. They prefer GICs and steady paycheques. And they love the 5-year fixed rate mortgage.

Others are quite comfortable with a higher level of variability in their lives. They can accept the ups and downs of equity investments. They may even accept variability in their incomes and be self-employed. And they are quite happy with a mortgage rate that fluctuates.

THE SIMPLE WAY TO MANAGE YOUR MONEY

In 1998 Manulife Financial introduced Canadians to a new way of managing debt and personal finances with the launch of Manulife One, an "all-in-one" banking product that combines a mortgage, line of credit, savings, and a traditional bank account. While it is not my objective to promote particular companies and products, it is almost impossible to speak about this idea without mentioning Manulife since no other product like it exists at this time.

For most Canadians, the financial picture includes a bank account, personal savings account, line of credit and mortgage. Their cash flows through their bank account – pay goes in, bill payments, cash withdrawals, and various debits go out. When extra cash is available, it goes into savings, albeit often temporarily. At regular intervals, money flows from the bank account to their mortgage and line of credit. When funds are tight, money is transferred from the line of credit into the bank account. We earn nothing on money sitting in our bank account, very little on savings and yet pay at least prime or more on our line of credit and mortgage, even when all of these accounts are at one institution. All this seems perfectly normal.

Manulife One eliminates all of these and leaves you with just one account – a debt of course for most. Pay goes in and your debt goes down. Bills are paid and cash withdrawn and your debt goes up. You no longer have money sitting idle in bank accounts or next to idle in a savings account. And you no longer need to watch account balances and move funds from one account to another to cover upcoming expenses. You can't do the wrong thing with your money, since you only have one thing you can do. In effect your bank account, savings account, mortgage and any other debts are all being given exactly the same interest rate treatment.

Why aren't the other banks doing this? Good question, one you should probably ask. I suspect it has a lot to do with bank profits. Just a guess.

These aren't absolutes, but rather a continuum. The answer to your mortgage question, and your investment choices, lies in understanding where you are on that continuum.

If we crunch the numbers, it's easy to show that with few exceptions in time, the variable rate mortgage produces the lowest cost of borrowing. Locking in to a higher rate has a **price.** If you are willing to pay the price, you have found your spot on the continuum.

Mortgage vs. RRSP

Until you have eliminated your personal debt it rarely makes sense to invest - with one possible exception: your RRSP.

One of the key objectives in long term planning is usually to maximize net worth. Reducing your $200,000 mortgage to zero is the same as leaving the mortgage as i and building an investment portfolio with a net after tax value of $200,000 The question then is which has a more significant effect on net worth – paying down your mortgage or investing in your RRSP?

The question ultimately boils down to one of returns. If you believe that you mortgage rate is going to exceed (or even equal) the long term rate of return on your RRSP, then the mortgage is probably the place to put any extra cash **On the other hand,** if you believe that you can earn a greater return in the RRSP, allocate your money there.

Let's suppose that you have a $200,000 mortgage, amortized over 20 years at a rat of 6%. Your RRSP investments will earn 7% and your marginal tax rate is 30% You currently have a balance of zero in your RRSP. We have a cash flow of $300 per month to direct either to the RRSP or the mortgage. Because the RRSP contribution is tax deductible, we will assume that the actual contribution mad is $428.67 which after tax will equal the $300 we have available. In order to keep the playing field level, let's also assume that we will assess net worth on an after tax basis, so we will consider the potential tax (at the same marginal rate) that wil have to be paid on the RRSP funds as they are withdrawn in the future.

Also, we will assume that if we direct the funds to our mortgage, when it is paid of we will direct the mortgage payment, plus the extra $300, plus the tax savings to ou RRSP from that point on.

Consider the outcome in 1, 5, 10 and 20 years.

SCENARIO 1: CONTRIBUTE $428.67 TO RRSP ($300 AFTER-TAX REFUND)

YEAR	1	5	10	20
RRSP Value (7% return)	$5,309	$30,610	$73,789	$220,615
Less: Tax payable on RRSP withdrawal	$1,593	$9,183	$22,137	$66,184
Less: Mortgage Balance	$194,615	$169,592	$128,727	$0
NET WORTH	-$190,899	-$148,165	-$77,075	$154,431

SCENARIO 2: CONTRIBUTE $300 TO MORTGAGE

YEAR	1	5	10	20
RRSP Value (7% return)	$0	$0	$0	$204,269
Less: Tax payable on RRSP withdrawal	$0	$0	$0	$61,281
Less: Mortgage Balance	$190,916	$148,701	$79,760	$0
NET WORTH	-$190,916	-$148,701	-$79,760	$142,988

For some people, the key point on this issue isn't mathematical, it's emotional. The question is, will you feel better getting rid of a big debt, or watching assets grow in your RRSP? Are you willing to invest in your RRSP in such a way as to outperform the cost of the mortgage?

Most people view their RRSP investments as "long term" and are more likely to invest in such as way as to earn higher returns. They are more likely to accept volatility as part of the equation, and remain invested during downturns thus ensuring that healthy long term returns are realized. Because of this long term viewpoint I believe that most RRSP accounts will in fact outperform the rates of long term debt, making the RRSP a clear winner in this debate. Still, some find a large debt a big burden to carry, and would prefer to do whatever it takes to get it reduced as quickly as possible.

There is however a solid compromise in this debate that more often than not satisfies the psyche of most financial personalities – do both. Take the $300 (not $428.67) and put it into the RRSP. Take the refund ($90) and apply it to the mortgage. Now **everybody's** happy.

Credit cards

There is no middle ground here. They are convenient and when used properly, actually provide a positive financial effect. All amounts charged to a credit card can be paid later at no cost, hence saving you interest charges, so long as you pay the full balance at month end. If you don't of course, high interest charges apply, making the credit card a losing proposition.

Never carry a balance. Never. **It's that simple.**

Getting out of debt

If you find yourself swamped in monthly payments and you appear to be sinking deeper each month, you may be looking for some ideas on how to get back onto dry land. Here are a few quick tips.

1. **Prepare a net worth statement.** If you haven't already, now would be a good time to get a fix on "where you are now." Often people feel a lot worse than they need to because they are looking at the details and not the big picture.

2. **Shift debts to the lowest rates.** Analyze all debts on the basis of cost (net cost if any are tax deductible). Wherever possible, move higher cost debt over to lower cost lenders. The perfect example of that of course is using a line of credit to pay off credit cards. **Do it.**

3. **Consolidate.** Several small payments feel a lot worse than one big payment even when they add up to the same thing. Usually of course, a consolidation loan will not only reduce the number of payments but also the total amount, and that real-

MEET ELISHA AND PARKER GRAHAM

Elisha and Parker consider themselves to be "normal" Canadians, struggling to raise 2 children, save for retirement and get out from under the burden of debt that has pursued them for far too long. Like many Canadians, they had a complex array of financial accounts that they had slowly accumulated over the years, including 3 bank accounts, a mortgage, a line of credit, and a number of credit cards – 3 of which were carrying balances.

Among my recommendations was consolidation. In fact, I suggested that they consolidate all of their banking products into a flexible mortgage account (Manulife One) in order to reduce interest payments and simplify their financial lives. Like many individuals who consider this strategy, they quickly concluded that eliminating the credit card debt with interest rates as high as 24% in favour of a debt at prime (at the time 3.75%) was an obvious advantage. Not so obvious was giving up their individual bank accounts and consolidation of the mortgage and line of credit which were already at prime. I suggested however that the multitude of accounts had contributed to their problems. They felt disorganized. And they were feeling the stress of moving money between accounts like some financial shell game. One account would eliminate both problems. They decided to give it a try.

A little over a year later I met with them to review their financial situation and noticed two positive outcomes from the consolidation strategy. First, they were clearly in a better financial position due to the interest rate savings and the advantages obtained by the fact that all available cash was being used to keep their debt at a minimum at all times. This of course was predictable based on financial modeling. Second, they were feeling far better about their overall financial situation, and it turns out this was a far more important benefit.

Parker was all smiles as he relayed to me how they felt about the track they were now on. "We had no idea how much stress had been caused by dealing with our finances in such a piecemeal fashion. I know this is saving us money, but that's not the real advantage. The great thing is we are more relaxed and that is far more valuable." When it comes to money, simple is better.

ly feels good. **But be careful** – consolidation isn't a "get out of jail free" card. You are still in debt. Don't start adding new debts or you may find yourself in a worse position with consolidation no longer an option to reduce the pain.

4. **Have a plan to get out of debt.** When exactly will you be out of debt? Most people eventually assume that they may be in debt forever. Decide that won't be you. Draw a map. Keep score. Make it a game and see if you can get ahead of your plan. Success in most things is a result of strong emotional attachment. So get emotionally involved. Start thinking about life without the burden of debt. It can be done. You can do it. **Get started.**

5. **Create a spending plan.** Spending got you into debt. Spending could keep you there indefinitely. Read Chapter 4 and resolve to change the direction of your financial future so that you become debt free. Small changes over the span of many years can make an enormous difference.

6. **Stop moving the goal posts.** One of the most powerful emotions that you need to combat is the attachment to the financial status quo. It has often surprised me to see people dig themselves out of a financially painful situation only to put themselves back in by moving to a more expensive house, adding a vacation property, buying a new car, etc. The stress of managing the finances has become part of their norm and so they are happy to jump in again in order to obtain something else that is perceived as valuable.

Summary

There are a lot of reasons why we take on debt. Some of them are reasonable, some are not. For the most part, only you can be the judge of which is which. But for the majority of us, a debt is a burden. It drags down our net worth and wears us down psychologically. If you have a real financial problem, chances are it's debt. And that is the bottom line.

If you are looking to simplify your finances and discover the extraordinary life, debt is probably not part of the equation. Getting out of debt may be the fastest route to where you actually want to be. For most people, a debt-free existence is practically unimaginable. Start imagining. Start planning. It's easier than you think.

It's better than you can imagine.

SIMPLE MONEY

Borrow as little as you can, and repay it as quickly as possible.

Debt that enables you to do something good – own a home, get an education – isn't "good," but it may be necessary.

Credit card debt is disastrous. Get rid of it. Avoid it.

Borrow to invest only if you are sure you can handle the risk. In most cases, borrowing to invest isn't necessary.

Have a plan to reduce and eliminate debt.

EXTRAORDINARY LIFE

Pay down debt or contribute to RRSP? Unless the debt is a real burden, invest in the RRSP – it's your ticket to the extraordinary life.

Imagine a debt free life. Extraordinary isn't it? Now move towards it.

Chapter 11

Money and children

Rather than worry about what you are teaching your children, worry about the example you are setting. In the end, that is the only lesson that will stick.

A brief historical perspective

Money has been around for a long time. What hasn't been around so long are concepts like vacations, leisure time, retirement, and earning a living. Increasingly, the "important" things in life have come to be things that involve money. No where is this more sharply evident than in the growing concern for higher education.

The early universities had little to do with earning money. They were created to expand critical thinking - to enable students to broaden their horizons by learning to read and write and understand the world around them. They aroused the curiosity of the scientist and stimulated the creativity of the artist. While some today pursue higher education with such noble purpose, society as a whole now views post-secondary education as a way to get ahead in an increasingly competitive world. Today's students specializing in the liberal arts such as philosophy or literature will invariably encounter the question: "How are you going to turn this education into an income?"

In a single generation, the emphasis placed on education has shifted enormously. Parents today worry about their child's future from the moment the child is born. Every effort is made to make sure that their child is the first to read, first to articulate complex concepts, first to understand mathematics, and first out the door of high school and on to university where the critical phase of developing earning power takes place. The rationale is clear: a good education leads to a good career generating a good income for **a good life.**

This is an issue that has escalated rapidly in the past 20 years, and it is common to throw around statistics that speak to the increasingly higher grades needed to secure entrance to Canada's universities, and more to the point, the dramatic increase in the cost of higher education.

What this ultimately amounts to for today's youth is pressure - pressure to excel, pressure to compete for positions, and pressure to earn the money to pay the way. Unlike their parents and grandparents, children today learn at a remarkably young age how to handle money, how to earn money, and how important money is in our lives – even if what they learn **isn't right.**

The Simple Lesson

There are two major issues when it comes to children and money. The first is how we can teach them to be good at managing money. The second is how we can best accumulate funds to cover the escalating costs of post-secondary education.

Teach your children well

If you want your children to enjoy a healthy relationship with money, to understand the value of money, how to attract and keep it, and how to use it to live an extraordinary life, there is only one thing you need to do: show them. Like it or not, your children will adopt your personality, your values, and your beliefs. So rather than worry about what you are teaching your children, worry about the example you are setting. In the end, that is the **only lesson** that will stick.

Bearing the costs of post secondary education

In the eyes of a parent, every new-born child is already headed to university. It is of course a parent's prerogative to see only the best in their child and to want only the best for their future. After all, a better education usually means a better life. Unfortunately a better education is getting more expensive with each passing year.

MEET BRENDA AND WALTER FLEMING

Brenda and Walter Fleming have a large family – eight children in all – ranging in age from 25 to 7. Walter is an electrician, and Brenda is a stay-at-home Mom. On most days Walter admits he has the easier job. Despite the challenge of squeezing the living expenses of ten people into one moderate income, both Walter and Brenda never complain, and in fact they have a cheery and optimistic perspecitve on money.

While it would be financially impossible for the Fleming's to make maximum contributions to an RESP each year, they nonetheless "save what they can," and have established accounts, either RESP or in-trust-for (ITF) accounts for all eight with the older ones already putting much of the money to good use.

What is most noteworthy about this family is the lesson they have taught me about money and family. The simplest way to understand it is to say they are all in it together. Brenda and Walter save what they can to help, but each child starts working in their teens and knows that some of the money they earn is going to be needed to put them through university. So far, all those who have graduated from high school have gone on to university, and through working and saving and the help provided from Mom and Dad, are doing just fine. The oldest two, both girls, Karen and Kristen, shared accommodation and transportation to university, a great cost saving strategy and I suspect a way of keeping some of home with them as they ventured out on their own.

Both Karen and Kristen have become clients of mine in their own right, and while working with me independently, they have exhibited the same perspective on money. They know what their needs are and those needs are easily met. Beyond that, they allocate some to savings (they actually contributed small amounts to their RRSP accounts while attending university) hoping to someday buy a house of their own. They spend some on recreation and travel, and they generally find a little available to help their younger siblings. Not surprisingly, dealing with them is almost like dealing with Walter and Brenda - always a real pleasure.

I spoke to Walter and Brenda about this and complimented them on raising such outstanding individuals who possess such a healthy attitude about money. Walter shared with me the secret, a lesson we can all apply. "We handle our money exactly as we tell them to handle theirs. What else could they learn?"

Exactly.

CHILDREN AND ALLOWANCE

Should you give children an allowance? Yes, when they show signs of needing and wanting some financial independence. Don't start until children understand that the allowance will replace the need for them to ask you for certain things – candy and toys for example. Allow them to experience that independence by giving them the freedom to spend their money as they please, without undue influence or judgment. This isn't about managing a budget - it's about teaching independence and giving children the freedom to experience who they are as individuals. Encourage them to save for bigger items and show them how, and if you want to influence those decisions, agree to share in the cost of those items you deem valuable to them.

For the average family, it is unlikely that post secondary education will become economically out of reach. Higher education is not only a family matter, it's a social issue as well, and while governments have no doubt been pushing more and more of the burden of tuition onto individuals, it is not in an effort to make higher education available only to the wealthy.

Still, it is a good idea to start saving for your children's education when they are young for many reasons. It puts the power of compounding to work for you. It takes advantage of tax deferral and income splitting. And for most parents, it's also psychologically soothing. But it's unhealthy to believe that this is a high priority for a newborn child, especially if the cost of saving puts a strain on the budget, or if the effort to save results in added stress.

The important thing here is this: do something, but keep it in perspective. With 17 years or more until funds are needed, surprisingly little can go a long way.

Putting the lesson to work

Our attitudes about money - the values, beliefs and judgements we impose on financial issues - are far from universal. Some see money as a necessary evil, others as the key ingredient in a system that rewards hard work and excellence. Some see money as secondary to job satisfaction, others as a primary motivator for each step on the career ladder. Some believe in saving and eliminating debt, others believe in spending in order to keep cash flowing and borrowing to increase wealth and life's experiences.

As always, there's no right and wrong. However, those in pursuit of simple money and an extraordinary life tend to share some common views on how money should be perceived. Often these people hope to pass those views on to their children. For those people, this is the ultimate opportunity to make dramatic changes to their own financial lives. Children bring with them a new and powerful kind of motivation to "do the right thing."

We must understand that it is impossible for us to teach our children one thing while living another. We can't tell our children to pursue a career based on their dreams, while at the same time complain that we hate our jobs but "hey, it's a paycheque." And so, teaching children what we want them to know about money means first learning the lessons ourselves, and then living them.

We all know the attributes of great children: confident, high self esteem, independent, respectful, curious, happy. **Money isn't responsible for any of these,** and yet lack of money is often blamed when any are missing.

Listen to the things you say to your children that give them clues to what money is all about. Try to avoid saying things like "we can't afford that," or "you kids are going to drive us to the poor house!" Instead say "I think there are better things to spend our money on," and "we are rich because we have you."

The number one financial gift that parents say they want to pass on to their children is a life without financial worries. Too often those same parents believe that this means either giving their children the means to earn a lot of money via an expensive education, or outright giving them money through gifts of cash on graduation, marriage, the purchase of the first house, or an inheritance. While there is nothing wrong with any of these strategies, they likely won't accomplish the desired outcome.

The only thing that will assure your children of living in harmony with money i. **experiencing that harmony** as they grow up.

Saving for baby's future

It's surprising, and sad, that quite early in the life of our child we start to worry even panic, about our ability to pay for a post-secondary education. The number do seem intimidating. The average cost of one year at university in Canada including room and board, is in excess of $13,000. If we assume that inflation wil increase those costs by 3% per year and that the student will attend university fo: 4 years beginning 17 years from birth, the total anticipated cost of educating a newborn is almost **$90,000.**

This may indeed be cause for concern, but proper planning requires perspective To that end, one needs to consider the other reasonable possibilities. It is quite possible that little Susie won't want and/or even need a post secondary education In fairness, how can we know what Susie will want, or even what education programs will cost in 17 or more years? Even if we are reasonably accurate in ou financial predictions (which is what we secretly hope), she may find a co-op program or get a part-time job that will allow her to work and go to schoo alternately, thus paying her own way or at least supplementing parental support Our own personal income and expenses will be different in 17 years and perhap. will allow us to fund more than we expect out of our income.

LIFE INSURANCE FOR YOUR CHILDREN'S EDUCATION

Life insurance agents will often pitch the idea of using permanent life insurance as a vehicle for sav ing money for children. Unless you already have or want to have permanent insurance in place fo some other purpose, the cost of the insurance, even on the life of a young child, is a sufficient drag on the savings to make this a less attractive strategy than an ITF account or an RESP. If you have seen a presentation that makes this idea look "too good to be true," it probably is.

The point is: trying to completely solve this problem at an early age is both unnecessary and fraught with uncertainties. The best thing to do is to understand what can be done, and then prioritize this item along with all the other financial issues currently on your plate.

Saving strategies

When it comes to actually saving funds for a child's education, there are two prominent strategies. The first is an "in-trust-for" (ITF) account, the second the government supported Registered Education Savings Plan (RESP). Let's take a closer look at each.

In-trust-for accounts

In this strategy, you are essentially giving money to your child and allowing that money to accumulate and grow in an account that you hold in trust for them. For the most part, these accounts are not set up with any legal documentation; they are not legal trusts, but rather "informal" trusts. In each ITF account there must be three parties: the beneficiary is the individual who will ultimately receive the funds (the child), the contributor is the individual who contributes funds (usually a parent), and the trustee is the individual who makes the investment decisions while the funds are accumulating (usually the other parent). To keep compliant with tax regulations, these three parties must be separate and distinct.

When funds are given to children, any interest income or dividend income earned from those funds continue to be taxed in the hands of the contributor. This means

BEWARE THE ATTRIBUTION RULES

When using an ITF account it is wise to separate third-party funds from the child's own funds by opening two accounts if necessary. The tax rules that require dividends and interest to be attributed back to the contributor will over time erode an ITF account's return. Those funds that are considered the beneficiary's to begin with, including government family allowances, gifts on birthdays and holidays, and of course earned income, will not be subject to this treatment.

that little is gained by using an ITF account if the investments are all interest bearing or dividend paying securities. But when funds given to children, (or to be technical, put into an ITF account) earn capital gains, those capital gains are taxed in the hands of the beneficiary, making this an **excellent income splitting strategy.**

Let's suppose for example that Jim and Sandra have a daughter Beth. Jim contributes $1,000 to an ITF account, with Sandra the trustee and Beth as beneficiary. Sandra decides to invest in a GIC earning 4% per year, so during the year, the account earns $40 in interest. When taxes are filed, Jim, as contributor, must claim the $40 of income on his tax return. If Jim is in the highest income tax bracket he will pay $18.40 in taxes, leaving $21.60 for Beth.

But if Sandra had instead invested in a mutual fund portfolio that would generate only capital gains or deferred capital gains as income, and if that fund had grown during the year by the same 4%, the account would now be worth $1,040. Unless Sandra sells the fund, no gain will be triggered and no tax will be payable, leaving the entire $40 in growth to begin compounding. But even if the fund had generated $40 in realized capital gains, or if Sandra had decided to sell the fund at year end and therefore triggered the capital gains of $40, the capital gains income would be reportable by Beth and not Jim. Presumably Beth isn't earning any other income, or even if she is working part time, not enough income to exceed the non-taxable level and therefore no tax would be payable.

Obviously investing to earn capital gains makes the most sense here, but Jim and Sandra should remember that investing this way is by definition going to be more volatile. They must be willing to withstand the ups and downs of the market, and must have a long enough time horizon so the portfolio can recover from any substantial downturns. As children get older and approach the age at which funds will be needed, it becomes increasingly difficult to justify such an aggressive allocation. There may come a time when the portfolio should shift to interest income. Some accounting may be necessary to determine the extent to which this income is allocated to Jim.

The **main advantage** of the ITF account over the RESP **is flexibility.** There is no restriction placed on the use of funds: funds can be turned over to the beneficiary at any time and subsequently used for any purpose. Technically, the funds become the property of the beneficiary at age 18 (to avoid that, a legal trust with differing terms would need to be established) at which time the beneficiary could demand ownership. Most families of course wouldn't experience any sort of financial mutiny at this juncture, **but one never knows.**

RESP

An RESP has two specific parties: the beneficiary is the child and eventual student, and the contributor is the individual putting money into the account.

The RESP is a program that provides financial assistance in two ways. The first $2,000 of contributions made to an RESP each year for each beneficiary receives a Canadian Education Savings Grant (CESG) equal to 20% of that contribution (the maximum grant each year is 20% of $2,000 = $400). Secondly, an RESP is considered a tax shelter, somewhat like an RRSP in that funds inside an RESP can earn interest, dividends or capital gains that will not be subject to tax. However, when funds are eventually withdrawn, tax is paid at that time. Income from an RESP must be reported as "other" income, and it will be taxed at the same levels as interest income.

WHAT SCHOOLS QUALIFY?

"What types of schools qualify as eligible institutions when my child decides to put the RESP funds to use?" The answer is "most of the schools that you would imagine." There is in fact no all-inclusive list, but rather a general guideline that includes all Canadian universities, colleges, technical schools as well as many foreign institutions, correspondence courses and probably whatever means of delivering educational services is implemented in the future. The intent is to assist Canadians in obtaining useful education and training at the post secondary school level, not to steer them into specific institutions favoured by RESP rules.

POOLED RESP ACCOUNTS

Pooled accounts, (sometimes called scholarship trusts), have been around for a long time and operat(
under the same general guidelines as an RESP. However, they also come with a long document out
lining the terms under which you must make contributions, and the terms under which you can with
draw funds, and for the most part, they make both much more restrictive. The upside, if any, is likel(
to come at the expense of someone else who has bailed on their contributions, or failed to qualify fo
educational withdrawals. For the most part, these contracts are confusing and poorly explained by sale.
people who seem far too eager to sign you up for a monthly subscription; essentially a commitmen(
that has no provision for stopping if funds become tight for you. Not all of these plans can be charac
terized in this rather negative light, but it's hard to tell the good from the bad. If you decide to use (
pooled account, read your contract carefully. How do you know if the product you are considering i
a pooled account? Probably the easiest way is this: if you have no choice in the investments, it's (
pooled account.

In understanding the various implications of an RESP, we need to distinguis(
between three separate pools of money within the RESP: the contributions, th(
CESG, and the growth.

Let's suppose that Jim and Sandra decide to establish an RESP for Beth, who i:
currently 2. For the next 16 years they contribute $2,000 to the RESP in order t(
obtain the maximum available grant each year.

Assuming a 6% average return each year, by the end of the 16th year, they wil
have $64,695 in the RESP comprised of $32,000 in contributions, $6,400 ir
CESG and $26,295 in growth. When the funds are withdrawn by Beth to func
her education, the growth portion and the CESG portion will be considered tax
able income to her in the year withdrawn. Note that the contributions are no(
considered taxable income as they were deposited as after-tax dollars by Jim.

If Sandra and Jim had made the same $2,000 contributions to an ITF accoun(
each year, and earned the same 6% growth rate (let's assume it was all capital gain.
– it will keep the math simpler), the account would be worth $54,426

Clearly, the RESP delivers more, thanks to the

CESG and the associated growth. Furthermore, the funds inside the RESP can be invested to earn interest or dividends without any potential drain due to taxation.

But, what if Beth doesn't use these funds for education?

In the case of the ITF account that simply means that Beth will have $54,426 to use for something else – perhaps a down payment on a home, to start a business, or fund a wedding. If the funds are in an RESP, however, it's a little more complicated. The funds considered contributions revert back to the contributor without consequence. The CESG funds revert back to the government. That leaves the growth portion of $26,295.

The RESP provisions allow for two possible solutions to avoid taxation. First, another blood relative may use the RESP funds to fund education expenses. Second, the growth portion may be transferred tax free into the contributors RRSP, provided they have the eligible RRSP room. Since it is poor planning to have this much room available, this is in fact a questionable strategy, and is unlikely to be viable when the time comes. Failing these strategies, the growth is then considered income to the contributor and is taxed at his marginal tax rate, and further penalized 20%. If Jim is in the highest tax bracket today he would pay $12,905 in tax, and suffer a $5,295 penalty, meaning that he would receive only $8,941 in net growth.

The final result in our worst-case scenario then is that the funds would shrink to $40,941 in the RESP while remaining at $54,426 in the ITF account. These numbers may leave some wondering which strategy is best.

So long as you remain confident, or hopeful, that your child will attend some sort of post-secondary educational program, **the RESP is clearly the best way to accumulate funds.** Keep in mind that funds can flow between siblings, increasing the odds of putting the money to its intended use. And accumulating funds in an RESP may in fact increase the

MEET DAN AND LESLIE VINNY

Dan and Leslie Vinny have two children; when we met, Michael was 1 and Samantha was 3. Since the birth of each child they had been utilizing the RESP, making every effort to maximize contributions each year to attract the government grants. They lived in an apartment, and one of their highest financial priorities was to buy their own place. Especially when Michael started walking they found the apartment confining and longed for something with a back yard they could call their own.

They were having a tough time saving, even with the part-time income that Leslie was earning, and Dan was actively looking for something to supplement his income as a customer service rep with a major insurance company. They had opened up RRSP accounts before Samantha was born, but hadn't contributed since; in fact they had taken funds out one year, and the current balances were less than $7,000 for Dan and only $2,000 for Leslie.

At our first meeting I challenged the logic that had them contributing almost $4,000 each year to fund education expenses that were some 15 to 17 years away and yet almost nothing to saving for a house. They had thought this through and were ready for my question. "We both agreed," explained Leslie, "that if we didn't make the children's education a priority we would get there and be unable to afford it. As soon as Sam was born, we made a promise to put the education savings first and work the rest of our finances around it."

A few weeks later I returned with a number of different financial models for them to consider. Based on our agreed-upon predictions of education costs, rates of return, other expenses and incomes, their future looked a lot better than they had expected. The financial model showed that based on present contributions to the RESP, they would almost entirely fund the anticipated education expenses. They both nodded and smiled as this reinforced the value of their current planning. But if they were going to get into a home of their own any time soon, they would have to cut current expenses in order to make room.

odds that your child will attend something beyond high school, since funding has been established.

At the same time, prudence suggests that RESP accounts be used in moderation. For example, although only the first $2,000 of contributions receives the government grant, annual contributions can in fact be as high as $4,000 per child. If you

Even when we considered accumulating $20,000 each inside their RRSP, using the tax deductible savings to speed up the process, the goal appeared out of reach.

Then we considered a scenario in which RESP contributions were suspended for the next 3 years, and the funds allocated to their RRSPs. Suddenly a down payment became feasible. The impact to the eventual RESP assets was considerable, but I tried not to impose my own values and merely pointed out that I wanted to be sure we had things in the proper priority. "At the moment," I said, "Your children's education is number one and owning a home is number two. If that's how it should be, then you are presently on the right track."

What happened after that could only be described as rationalization. The conversation moved from the possibility that they could increase savings in the future to "catch up," to giving reasonable consideration to the fact that the children themselves may be able to contribute to their own educational expenses when the time comes. Leslie said, "You know, the house is as much for the children as it is for us. We want them to grow up in a home. It's crazy not to make the house purchase our number one priority. And it looks like right now, there just isn't room for number two."

Sometimes we need to save a portion of our present resources in order to prepare for future needs, and sometimes we need to pull back those resources allocated to the future to realize the extraordinary life we deserve today. Only by looking at the big picture in a simple and organized way are we able to make those decisions with clarity.

That was 4 years ago. The Vinnys move into their first home later this year. And according to Leslie and Dan, life couldn't be better.

are attempting to catch up on previously unused years to capture the grant big contributions make sense. Otherwise, adding funds to the RESP without attracting the grant, where growth may eventually be subject to a severe penalty, doesn't make sense, unless it is a **near certainty** that your child will in fact attend university or college.

A combination of both types of accounts might make the most sense

in cases where there is more than one child and there is some uncertainty regarding the use of funds. In cases where complete flexibility is desired, or post secondary schools appear to be a more remote possibility, the ITF account is best.

For most people, the key is to just do something, and most are surprised at how far a little each month can go. A small contribution of $100 per month for 18 years at 6% results in $38,735 in an ITF account, or $46,482 in an RESP. Without question, that will be a welcome helping hand to your young student and considerable relief to you when faced with a large tuition bill.

Set aside an amount each month or each year that won't jeopardize your other priorities and establish a simple strategy that makes sense to you. Your child's future is indeed important, and you want for them every opportunity available. Balance the needs for their future along with the family's needs today, and you will experience an extraordinary life **together.**

SIMPLE MONEY

The only way to teach your children about money, is to set an example.

If you want flexibility in how money is spent, use an In-trust-for account to save for you child.

If you want to maximize the dollars you accumulate specifically for post secondary education, use an RESP.

EXTRAORDINARY LIFE

Your child's extraordinary life doesn't start when they graduate from university, it starts the day they are born. Balance saving for their education, and family life today accordingly.

Chapter 12

Getting help

A good advisor will help you simplify your financial life, and inspire you to lead the life you really want – a life that's extraordinary. That's someone worth searching for.

A brief historical perspective

More change has occurred in the financial services industry in the last 20 years than in the previous 200 years. Until the mid 1980s, the industry was neatly divided into banks, insurance companies, and stockbrokers. Other than slinging mud at each other's products and services, rarely did these distinct groups interact.

In the 80s and 90s, a flurry of new products and a long-running bull market acted as catalysts for accelerating change. The birth of money market funds - low risk interest paying investments - allowed stockbrokers to steal assets from the banks. Mutual funds, which were growing rapidly, were a perfect fit for the personal selling skills of life insurance agents, and segregated funds and asset-based life insurance products like Universal Life saw the insurance industry stealing assets away from the stockbrokers. The stockbrokers countered by licensing reps to sell insurance. And the banks gobbled up the stockbrokers, incorporating them into their branches, and now stand on the doorway of the life insurance companies hoping to do the same.

While this product-based war was being waged, another group began to emerge – Financial Planners. Barely noticed before 1990, Financial Planners shifted the focus away from product and onto planning. Rather than having your banker, insurance agent and stockbroker playing tug of war for your dollars, financial planners promised to provide unbiased advice and assistance in all areas of your financial life.

The problem is, it's hard to tell if that promise is actually being fulfilled. Most of the people who call themselves financial planners are in fact long-standing members of one of the original three camps. Life insurance agents, bank employees, and stockbrokers need to do little more than create a few projections, call it a plan, and they can legitimately call themselves financial planners, all the while focusing their attention on the sale of the product that will pay them the most commission. This is the concern of critics – sometimes with good cause – that is today at the heart of the effort to bring standards to an industry whose regulatory structure is, for the most part, still operating under the bank-insurance-stockbroker paradigm.

And so today, the consumer who goes looking for a "financial advisor," is indeed in a **confusing** position. First, there is an almost endless range of advisor types. At one extreme are those who create financial plans on a fee-for-service basis and sell no financial products. At the other extreme are those who sell product only, offering nothing in the way of a financial plan. In between, where the vast majority of financial advisors are found, are those who mix advice giving and product selling – raising questions about the potential conflict of interest.

In case this sounds like a hopeless situation, let me assure you, it's not. **It's difficult, but not impossible** to find a good financial advisor – someone who offers truly objective advice, someone who you can trust to help you navigate the often stormy seas of your financial life. Let's discuss how.

The Simple Lesson

First of all, I'm assuming that you in fact want a financial advisor. Not everyone needs or wants one, and I'm not suggesting here that everyone should work with one. There are some Canadians who are quite content steering their own financial boat. They have the time, the interest, and the ability to develop their own plans, evaluate financial products and manage their own investments. These people are few in number, but **they do exist.**

CONDUCT INTERVIEWS

One of the first rules of hiring staff is make sure you hire from a pool of candidates. In other words, don't hire the first person who walks through the door. This is an excellent rule to keep in mind when looking for a financial advisor. Unfortunately, it's a rule that is rarely followed.

The problem is pretty simple: successful advisors are successful because they are good at attracting new clients. They make a good first impression. They have a good pitch, complete with fancy brochures, testimonial letters, samples of their work and other convincing materials all designed to do one thing – to stop you from looking elsewhere for an advisor.

You are not looking for a "successful" advisor, you are looking for a comprehensive, competent, committed and compatible advisor. And you're not going to find out about the compatible part unless you do some digging past the marketing hype that is staged for the first meeting.

In order to find the best advisor for you, it is imperative that you meet several. At those meetings you must ask questions that help you get to really know these people. Ask questions that bump them off the sales track they are likely to try to stay on. Ask them about personal things – how they spend vacations, and what hobbies they have. Ask them to tell you about their family. These types of questions will tell you much more about what's important to them – about their values.

Ask them how they got into the business of financial planning, and why. This will tell you more about previous experience that may be relevant, or perhaps dangerous. It will also speak of their passion and the likelihood of staying in the business, and hence your advisor, for a long time.

Ask them to support why they believe that money should be managed in the way they recommend. Look for belief that stems from personal understanding, as opposed to blindly following a system imposed on them by a supporting company or manager. This is your interview, so you should run the show. Ask any question you feel is helpful in the process of getting to know someone. Be curious. Dig for reasons.

Your goal in finding an advisor is to find someone who will take an interest in your life. You want your advisor to help you discover the strategies and plans that will make your life extraordinary. And then work with you over the years to come to help you realize more than you thought possible.

REFERRALS

Most experts will tell you that the best way to find a good advisor is to find a friend or relative who is happy with their advisor. I agree - to a point.

Referrals are indeed a good place to start. But it's important to note that just because you are friends with someone, or even related to someone, that does not mean you share the same financial personalities. Nor does it necessarily mean you would be happy with the same advisor. Furthermore, most people want to believe that they have chosen the absolute best advisor and so their claims of excellence may be unintentionally bloated. Add these advisors to your interview pool, but don't assume that you've found the one just because Uncle Bob says his advisor is the best guy on the planet.

There are others perhaps who are able to manage their investments, but are not at all interested in insurance and estate planning, or who would like some help developing an overall financial plan. These people want guidance in some areas, and reassurance in others. And they don't want to pay for advice they don't need.

The important thing is this: Determine what kind of help you need, and go looking for it. Make it clear to prospective advisors what it is you want, and be aware – they may try to up sell you on the importance of something other than what you were looking for. Exercise caution, and use good judgement.

For the sake of this book I'm going to stick to the idea that a key step to simplifying your life is getting good help – with respect to money, comprehensive help. If your goal is to live an extraordinary life without spending unnecessary time worrying about your investments, or your financial plan, then a comprehensive financial planner is what you need.

Let's imagine what this ideal advisor would look like, and while excellent advisors come in both genders and have many names, let's call our ideal advisor **Alice.**

Alice has some experience which has demonstrated that she knows how to do her job. She insists that before she can help you determine how to invest, how much to save, what kind of insurance you should have, etc., that she must create a financial plan with you – a plan that will serve as a backdrop for all financial decisions both now, and at each stage of your life.

She has the right qualifications to do this – a CFP designation (Certified Financial Planner) at least – and she continues to study in order to remain up-to-date on new strategies. More importantly, Alice knows that your financial plan is based on the future you imagine (or want to imagine) for yourself. **Your dreams, your goals, your life –** this is what forms the basis of your financial plan.

Even though she may enlist the help of others for specific products, Alice remains involved, helping you make all of your financial decisions. She agrees to work with you personally, and remains your personal advisor for many years, likely decades - she doesn't pass you off to a junior associate shortly after taking you on as a client so that she can work with her more important clients (those who are making her more money). You find Alice inspiring, and you find yourself compelled to take her advice, even when it appears to go against your gut reaction. She is calm and sensible. You like her, you trust her, and over time your experience shows that she truly has your best interests at heart.

The essence of Alice the advisor can be summed up by highlighting **the four "Cs":** comprehensive, competent, committed, and compatible. That's the type of person you're looking for.

Putting the lesson to work

Let's look at each of the characteristics and consider how one may search for those traits.

Comprehensive

The comprehensive planner will help you to articulate your life dreams, and from them, create an overall financial plan or road map. She will assist you in implementing that plan to realize all of your dreams, and be there at every step to answer your questions and find the right solutions and products for **you.**

Your plan will likely cover cash flow, retirement savings, investment strategies, risk management, estate planning, educating children, and debt management. The recommended steps for implementation should complement each other, working together to achieve your goals.

There are critics who suggest that this type of planner, who might reasonably be called a generalist, may lack the necessary skills to help you with the more sophisticated investment or estate planning strategies. Perhaps this is true. But the ideal planner is aware of this and takes the appropriate steps to fill those gaps. They recommend investment managers, estate planning specialists, and whatever type of specialist is required to put the best possible solutions into place. Together with you, they monitor and evaluate these individuals on an ongoing basis. You have an ally and an advocate - a quarterback, if you will - someone who speaks the same language as the specialist to assist you at every step. That's the best way you can continue to keep money simple (and life extraordinary).

How do you find a comprehensive advisor? Ask potential advisors these **three questions:**

1. **"What is your specialty?"** If the answer includes reference to a product, such as "I specialize in high end life insurance solutions," then you're on the wrong track. Look for answers that incorporate the idea of helping people live extraordinary lives – although these exact words might not be used.

2. **"How do you get paid?"** Compensation for advisors can be complicated. If an advisor charges a fee to complete a financial plan he is considered unbiased, but for many, the fee is rather large, making this method more attractive to the wealthy. Furthermore, if the fee-based planner is going to truly remain objective then he won't assist you in the selection and ongoing management of the various

financial products that you will need to follow the steps of the plan. On the other hand, if an advisor does not charge a fee for a plan, but instead gathers compensation in the form of commission from financial products, his objectivity is drawn into question. So, which approach should you go with? Either one can work. What's most important is that you understand how an advisor/planner makes money, and feel comfortable that this arrangement is fair and forms the basis of a solid, long-term relationship. Look for an advisor who himself is comfortable with his method of compensation and willing to discuss it openly.

3. **"Tell me about your network of specialists.** Who helps you when you need it, and who else am I likely to meet over the years if I work with you?" The possible list should include such people as investment managers, tax and estate experts, (likely lawyers and accountants), and insurance experts, especially in areas like disability or critical illness. Then ask about the experience and qualifications of these experts. Why them rather than someone else?

Competence

Obviously no one wants an incompetent advisor. The question is, how can you tell if an advisor is competent before you have taken the plunge and learned through experience?

Credentials obviously help. In Canada, the Certified Financial Planner designation (CFP) has become the most recognized indication of expertise in financial planning, and if your advisor doesn't have it, you should probably keep looking. If they have something else, ask about its relevance.

You should also ask to see examples of their work – financial plans, investment portfolios and other recommendations. **This is especially important** if you are paying a fee up front to have a financial plan prepared.

Unfortunately, the real test of competency is often the actual work that is done for you, so it's wise to move in stages with a new advisor. Start with the financial plan, and if that appears to be lacking, stop there and start looking for another planner before you start moving investments or setting up other financial products.

Keep in mind that the competence you are seeking is comprehensive. Many advisors will be highly competent in one area, be that life insurance, portfolio management, etc. You want competence across the spectrum of financial planning issues. If the focus of your meetings steers too often in one direction, it might be time to **take your business elsewhere.**

Commitment

Over time you will realize that the key to your relationship with a financial advisor is that it is just that – a relationship. There must be mutual trust, respect, and understanding. That can't happen unless both you and your advisor make a commitment to that relationship.

Your advisor's commitment should be exhibited in a number of ways. They need to see you as a whole person, not just numbers on spreadsheets and money in the bank. This will be most evident in the kinds of questions they ask you when drafting or revisiting your financial plan. The committed advisor will show greater curiosity – asking questions that begin with why, wondering how you feel, and prodding deeper when something appears hidden. If you suggest you would like to retire as soon as possible, a committed advisor will immediately begin probing, looking for unhappiness on the job, or a strong desire you might have to do something else, like pursue a hobby or a new career.

An advisor should also make the commitment to work with you on an ongoing basis, and explain at the outset if you are likely to be passed off to an assistant once the initial business is complete. You don't need to have your advisor visiting you on some sort of schedule, but you would like to know that when help is needed, the advisor who has become familiar with your situation and your personality will be on hand to assist.

ADVISORS AND THE MEDIA

It's safe to say that the press is generally biased against the financial advisor community. Let's face it, the story about the advisor who milked his clients – all of whom are over 80 and now destitute – is compelling news. The story of the advisor who quietly helps clients get on the right financial track and live extraordinary lives, well, that's just not interesting.

The media is often quick to line up against advisors with headlines that shout, "Why pay fees to an advisor when you can buy the same fund on your own for much less!" Indeed, how hard can it be to pick funds? A number of experts publish annual reports on the top funds, and rating services apply 5 stars to those that should find their way into your portfolio. Right?

The key to success here is not the investments you choose, but your willingness to stay on board when they no longer look like the best. You don't really need help choosing (arguably a one time event), you need help to stop yourself from switching those choices on a regular basis – the single biggest reason that investors more often than not underperform the investments they own.

More importantly, financial planning means a lot more than picking the right investments. Investing, after all, is just one piece of the financial puzzle. A puzzle, that for many grows increasingly complex while simultaneously growing in importance.

Helping you put that puzzle together, and continually ensuring that all of the pieces work seamlessly to create the picture of the extraordinary life you want to live – that's what you pay for, and that's what you should be getting from a truly great financial advisor.

And finally, your advisor needs to put your interests ahead of their own, and point out to you situations in which that may prove difficult. This is included in most of the "codes of ethics" of the various associations that advisors may belong to – but of course that doesn't provide any guarantee. In the end, people of integrity do this naturally, and people who lack integrity break the code anyways. Look for indicators that this is an important issue to your advisor. Ask them specifically how they make sure this happens. If they point to a mission statement, get them to give you examples of how that mission statement is brought to life in their work.

ALPHABET SOUP

In an industry undergoing nearly constant change, ongoing education is extremely important. While not all valuable education an advisor receives contributes to the alphabet soup you may find on business cards, there are nonetheless a number of designations that may help you to understand the background, capabilities and ongoing training, which a potential advisor has undertaken. Here are the important ones.

CFP – CERTIFIED FINANCIAL PLANNER

The only internationally recognized designation in financial planning, recognized in 18 countries.

Regulated by: Financial Planners Standards Council – a not-for-profit organization created in 1995 to develop, promote and enforce the highest standards of financial planning.

Supported by: The Financial Advisors Association of Canada (Advocis); The Canadian Institute of Chartered Accountants; The Canadian Institute of Financial Planning; Certified General Accountants Association of Canada; Certified Management Accountants of Canada; and Credit Union Institute of Canada.

Requirements: Six courses (420 to 600 hours of work, usually taking 2 – 4 years to complete)

Ongoing: 30 hours of qualified education each year

Relevance: Broad knowledge of financial planning

RFP – REGISTERED FINANCIAL PLANNER

Regulated by: Institute of Advanced Financial Planners (IAFP) – an organization formed in 2002 when the Canadian Association of Financial Planners (CAFP) merged with the Canadian Association of Financial and Insurance Advisors (CAIFA) in an effort to preserve their focus on providing the highest standard of financial planning to Canadians.

Requirements: "Submitting a high-quality, complex and comprehensive financial plan for peer review and successfully completing a comprehensive examination based on the application of financial planning expertise to a complex case." (From the IAFP website.) Three years of practical experience is also required.

Ongoing: 30 hours of qualified education each year

Relevance: Broad knowledge of financial planning

PFP – PERSONAL FINANCIAL PLANNER

Regulated by: Institute of Canadian Bankers
Requirements: Five courses (270 hours), six months apprenticeship
Ongoing: None
Relevance: Broad knowledge of financial planning

CLU – CHARTERED LIFE UNDERWRITER

Regulated by: Advocis – an organization formed by merging CAIFA and CAFP in 2002, and "...a national professional association that prepares, promotes and protects advisors in the public interest. We do this by providing a professional platform, including career support, designations, best practices direction, education, timely information and professional liability insurance. This strengthens the relationship of trust and respect between financial advisors and their clients, the public and government." (From the Advocis website)
Requirements: Seven courses (210 hours).
Ongoing: 60 hours of qualified education every two years
Relevance: Advanced knowledge in life insurance and estate planning

CHFC – CHARTERED FINANCIAL CONSULTANT

Regulated by: Advocis
Requirements: Three courses beyond CLU (90 additional hours)
Ongoing: Same as CLU - 60 hours of qualified education every two years.
Relevance: Broad knowledge in financial planning

RHU – REGISTERED HEALTH UNDERWRITER

Regulated by: Advocis
Requirements: Two courses (60 hours)
Ongoing: 30 hours of qualified education each year
Relevance: Advanced knowledge in disability insurance and critical illness, often referred to together as "living benefits."

Compatibility

Of all the criteria discussed here, this is the most important, and for most people, the easiest to assess.

Obviously, you should like your advisor.

If you don't, it's unlikely you will share with them the kind of information they need to truly be of assistance. If you are like most people, you tend to like people who have similar philosophies and values. This is an important consideration when it comes to choosing a financial advisor.

Particularly when it comes to investing, you need to agree with the underlying philosophy that your advisor applies. Let me give you an example.

In the Henson family, Randy makes all the investment decisions. His wife, Lauren, admits that she is simply uninterested, while Randy on the other hand enjoys selecting and monitoring the investments in their growing portfolio. When I first met the Hensons, Randy was unhappy with his recent returns. The technology meltdown had been particularly harsh on their more aggressive portfolio and he wondered if he needed a new advisor, and a new philosophy.

After reviewing a financial plan I had constructed, our attention turned to investing. Randy's interest in the meeting increased. I outlined my philosophy (well covered in Chapter 5) and looked for a response. Lauren was very complimentary, suggesting that she was completely comfortable with my recommended strategy, and felt she understood investing for perhaps the first time. Randy looked pensive and stated that perhaps this was the strategy that he needed to work towards.

Over the next 2 years Randy and I spoke often. Randy wanted to be involved, to assist in the ongoing analysis of the portfolio, and to "do something" on a regular basis. He simply didn't feel comfortable with my leave-it-alone strategy, and finally one day he told me that they were moving their account to another advisor – a stock broker in fact. I realized that Randy's personality required more involvement and more action.

Looking back, I should have known from the beginning. Randy and I were simply not compatible. **And that's ok.** This is a business relationship, and both parties have to feel comfortable doing business with the other for the relationship to work. The lesson here for you is this: look for an advisor who shares your underlying philosophy about money management. You may think you don't have a philosophy – but if a prospective advisor's strategy doesn't resonate with you in a positive way, **keep looking.**

It may sound over the top, but in the end, you are looking for an advisor who will **inspire you.** A good advisor will ask you about your most important dreams,and then based on those dreams, build a financial road map that will take you there. Along the way, there will be pot holes, you may get sidetracked, and occasionally hills will appear too difficult to climb. Those are the times that your advisor will be of most value to you. He will inspire you to continue, to get back on track, by reminding you of the dreams you have shared, and pointing out that the step you need to take – the next step – is easily within reach.

A good advisor will help you simplify your financial life, and inspire you to lead the life you really want – a life that's extraordinary.

That's someone worth searching for.

SIMPLE MONEY

Determine what kind of help you are looking for, and look for an advisor that provides that kind of help. Most people reading this book will be looking for a comprehensive financial advisor.

You want a competent advisor – look for designations, samples of work, and happy clients. And keep checking as the relationship unfolds.

You want an advisor who is committed to you and your relationship – an advisor who sees you and treats you as a whole person, and one whose long term business plans involve keeping you as a client.

You want an advisor who is compatible. Ask personal questions in an attempt to determine values, philosophies and beliefs. Do they line up with yours?

Interview more than one advisor.

Referrals are a good start, but not the end of the search.

EXTRAORDINARY LIFE

A good advisor will inspire you. Inspiration is essential to the extraordinary life.

Chapter 15

Money, inspiration, and the extraordinary life

There may be many sections of this book that would cause one to wonder: what does this have to do with an extraordinary life? In many cases the answer is simultaneously **nothing, and everything.**

Most of us are tangled up with money in ways that are unproductive. So often what we do, what we have, who we are and what we strive to be are defined by the money we have or believe we can have. We have given money a power it doesn't deserve – the power to define our lives.

Money is indeed a powerful motivator. Manifesting as fear and greed, it drives us to desperate acts, and torments us with a perpetual display of what might be, if only.

But in fact, what we seek is one thing that money won't provide.:

Inspiration.

The word inspire comes from the latin word inspirare_which means "to breathe upon or into." In its earliest usages, including Homer, it generally meant "the breath of God."

When we are inspired, we have the feeling of new life. We are renewed, invigorated, enthused and self-motivated to pursue something, someone, some experience - always with passion. Inspiration is what we crave the most and may indeed be the seed of the extraordinary life.

In Psychology 101 you learn of Maslow's hierarchy of needs. Maslow argued that our lives move through stages, and we are unable to move up to the next level until we satisfy the level below it. His hierarchy is as follows:

6. Self-transcendence (spiritual needs)
5. Self-actualization (being needs)
4. Self-respect (esteem needs)
3. Love & affection (belonging needs)
2. Security / safety (safety needs)
1. Food & water (physiological needs)

Without deliberating too much on what constitutes an item in each category, it isn't difficult to argue that inspiration belongs on the top half, and money on the bottom. In short, money (or more accurately lack of money) is often what **blocks our path** towards satisfying the needs of our being, and even our spirit.

If you are worried about where the money is going to come from for your next meal, it is quite probable that you are not devoting a lot of time to "realizing your full potential" as a human being, or to pursuing those things that inspire you.

True, most readers of this book will not be worried about paying the rent. But we get caught in a similar trap when we focus all of our attention on material things, whether these are the basics of living, or the house in the country that is just beyond our current financial grasp. Others spend so much time worrying about a distant future, saving every penny for the proverbial rainy day, that living today is overlooked.

The simple lesson is this: more often than not, our focus on money becomes a roadblock, a distraction that prevents us from pursuing our true goals. We become slaves to our need for more. Our life becomes a quest for a better paying job, a better investment, lower costs, a tax reduction, or a get-rich-quick scheme.

We dive into money, with all its mysteries and complexities, and hope that by focusing on money we will find a way to be able to forget about it.

We won't.

The preceeding chapters aren't about getting more money, they're about thinking **less** about it. My belief is that by seeing the various tools we use, such as financial plans, investments, and insurance, for what they are – tools – you will see that in fact more tools or even better tools is not what you need.

So, what do you need in order to live the extraordinary life? What should you be spending your time on, if not money? That's easy: **whatever inspires you.**

There are many things we do because we are motivated to do them. We go to work in the morning because we are motivated to pay our bills. We do our laundry and clean our houses because we are motivated to live in cleanliness. We make dinner because we are motivated to satisfy our hunger.

What do you do because you are inspired? What do you do with passion and enthusiasm, not because of some external need, but simply because you want to? What may jump to mind are things like climbing a mountain, playing a favourite sport, writing a book, walking in nature, traveling the world, working for a cause that's important to you.

The world around us is filled with stories of those who are successfully pursuing their inspiration – world class athletes, authors, actors, and others – most of whom we look to for inspiration ourselves. If your passion is big, your story may also one day be found among the famous. But I'm not just talking about these larger-than-life dreams. **I'm talking about all dreams.**

Your inspiration may be a child, a spouse, parent, or friend. You may find yourself with a desire simply to serve – many, or just one. And the fact is, you may find inspiration in virtually everything you do now. Consider for a moment a different perspective on your regular routine. You get up and go to work in the morning because you are inspired to help your company achieve its mission. You are inspired to do your laundry and clean your house because you want to serve your family, the people you love the most, among them, yourself. You are inspired to make dinner because you want the feeling of a healthy body – for you and those you are privileged to prepare a meal for.

It truly is a matter of **perspective.**

And when it comes to money, this perspective is easily and quickly clouded in a haze of fear, greed, and confusion.

Hopefully, the preceeding chapters have helped you to understand more about the various financial tools that you have available to help you in your pursuit of the extraordinary life. These tools are no doubt valuable, indeed in some cases critical, to achieving many of the dreams and goals that will become your extraordinary future. **But they alone won't do the job.** And if you spend too much time on your tools, nothing will get done – just as the carpenter who spends all of his time sharpening his saw will never build a house.

You need to discover what inspires you, and pursue it. This is truly the secret to an extraordinary life.

Let me summarize here by leaving you with seven steps to take towards your own extraordinary life.

1. **Know the answer to the question: what inspires you?** This is a remarkably simple question that is for most, remarkably hard to answer. Many will refer to this as your "calling." It may be described as a voice within that we often silence in our pursuit of material things. You will know what inspires you by how you feel. You will feel exhilaration, fulfillment, pride, joy, and a sense of purpose when following those things that truly inspire. You should make a list - write them down. Add, delete and make changes to your list often. But most importantly, find more and more ways to pursue those things on your list.

2. **Create a vision of your ideal future.** Read Chapter 2 again. Using the answer to "what inspires you?" create your future. This is the secret to getting what you want.

3. **Think abundance.** This book is not about helping you to be happy with less. You were born to live in abundance. If you are truly going to live an extraordinary life, and pursue those things that inspire you, you must realize that whatever you can imagine, you can achieve. Whatever you can picture in your mind, you can have. Whatever image of yourself you can hold in your thoughts, you can become. Don't think small. Think **abundance.**

4. **Put money in perspective – keep it simple.** Organize your financial life. Create a financial plan and follow it. Make financial decisions and move on. Most importantly, use money as a tool to get what you want.

5. **Get help, or decide, firmly, not to.** One of the easiest ways to reduce the time spent focused on money is to delegate certain money issues to a trusted advisor. Find one. Or, understand that you are in fact a "do-it-yourselfer" when it comes to money (just like some people actually repair their own cars), and waste no time looking for an advisor to agree with your every decision. In either case, put this issue to rest.

6. **Let go of all negative thoughts and feelings.** The secret to the universe may indeed be in understanding the elusive term "let go." Always speak, and think, in positive terms. When it comes to money, think about what you do want, not what you don't want. For example, "I want my money to outlive me," not "I don't want to run out of money." This is a remarkably simple concept. And yet, our reaction to negative outcomes in our lives leads to an enduring focus on the things we don't want, trapping us in the perpetual realization of that very thing. Break free. Let go. The universe is conspiring to give you what you want. Be sure your thoughts – the way you communicate what you want to everyone and everything around you – is clear.

7. **Be generous.** This is both a shortcut and the ultimate outcome. As each extraordinary life unfolds, individuals eventually realize that life is in fact abundant. There is more of everything, including money, than we need or could even possibly use in a lifetime. Giving it away becomes increasingly easier. And yet giving it away, surprisingly, leads to acquiring more with even more ease. At all stages of life, acceleration of the abundant life is simple - give more to others. Give freely, without expectation. More of everything including money, and inspiration, will naturally follow. The greatest discovery of this will be the realization that an extraordinary life is not one in which you rise above your family, friends, peers, and community.

It is one in which you all rise together.

Don't look through the pages of this book for inspiration. Look inside yourself. You were born with the blueprint of an extraordinary life inside you. Hopefully, you now see money as one of many tools available to help you build that life.

I wish you much joy and happiness in discovering and realizing the many wonders that life holds in store for you. And keep your money simple, so that

all your days will be
extraordinary.

About the author

A 20-year veteran of the financial services industry, Bill Bell is an author and financial professional based in Newmarket, Ontario.

Bill started his financial career in 1984 with the Paul Revere Life Insurance Company, after working for several years as a high-school math teacher. He quickly rose through the ranks until he was named General Manager of the company's Toronto operations, a position he held for six years.

In 1996, Bill left the executive suite to found his own financial planning practice. Since that time, he has helped hundreds of client families achieve their financial dreams through a disciplined approach to financial planning that offers clarity and peace of mind.

A graduate of both the University of Waterloo and Brock University, Bill holds a number of financial designations, including Certified Financial Planner (CFP), Chartered Life Underwriter (CLU), and Registered Health Underwriter (RHU).

Bill is an accomplished author, having published dozens of articles for newspapers and magazines on a variety of personal finance topics. He is a frequent guest on television and radio programs, and has been the keynote speaker at a number of financial education events. His first book, *One Step to Wealth,* was published in 1999 to critical acclaim.

Bill resides in Newmarket, Ont. with his wife Ellen and their three daughters, Leah, Deandra, and Alexis.

Contact the author

For more information on the topics we've discussed in *Simple Money,* please visit the book's website: **www.simplemoney.ca.**

There, you'll find a number of supporting articles and supplementary information that will add greater depth to the discussion in the book.

If you have a specific question or comment about any of the topics in *Simple Money,* or if you'd like to discuss how you can become a client, feel free to contact me at the following email address: **billbell@bellfinancial.ca** I'll do my best to get back to you in a timely manner – usually within a couple of days.

Please understand, however, that by its very nature, financial planning is a highly *personal* endeavour. Without sitting down with you and discussing the details of your personal financial situation, your financial goals, your tolerance for risk – in other words, without you becoming a *client* – it's impossible for me to provide you with detailed investment or planning advice.

I would be happy to visit your company or organization to deliver an informative and entertaining key-note presentation or seminar. For a list of topics and other information about this, please visit our website or contact us as outlined below:

23rd Street Press
15165 Yonge Street, Suite 201
Aurora, ON L4G 1M2
905-713-3765 | 1-888-367-7450
email: billbell@bellfinancial.ca
www.bellfinancial.ca | www.simplemoney.ca